NO HOPE FOR NORMAL

FRANCESCA BORELLA

909·books

No Hope For Normal by Francesca Borella
978-1-962702-00-3 Paperback
978-1-962702-01-0 Ebook

909 Books Collective staff: Mark Givens and Cati Porter
Cohort One: Francesca Borella and Dr. Jacqueline Mantz Rodriguez
Edited and produced by the 909 Books Collective
Cover art by Francesca Borella and Mark Givens

FIRST EDITION

Library of Congress Cataloging-in-Publication Data

Names: Borella, Francesca, 1956- author
Title: No hope for normal / Francesca Borella.
Identifiers: LCCN 2025018227 (print) | LCCN 2025018228 (ebook) | ISBN 9781962702003 paperback | ISBN 9781962702010 ebook
Subjects: LCSH: Borella, Francesca, 1956- | Parents of transgender children--United States--Biography | Families--United States--Biography | LCGFT: Autobiographies
Classification: LCC HQ759.9147 .B67 2026 (print) | LCC HQ759.9147 (ebook)
LC record available at https://lccn.loc.gov/2025018227
LC ebook record available at https://lccn.loc.gov/2025018228

WWW.909BOOKS.COM

ADVANCE PRAISE FOR NO HOPE FOR NORMAL

In *No Hope for Normal*, Francesca Borella's heartfelt, self-deprecating and often humorous memoir, the journey of self-discovery begins in a place of severe anger and frustration; as the book opens, Borella learns that her youngest child has realized they are trans and want to commence hormone therapy. Told in flashback vignettes, the book makes the reader Borella's willing travel companion on an alternatingly heartrending and comical quest for "normal." Readers will come along on a variety of adventures, ranging from baton twirling tryouts and a trip to the Emmy awards to the far-flung locales of Madagascar and Brazil, all with children, and a series of love-interests and husbands. Throughout, Borella uses her keen insights as a career anthropologist to makes sense of her own life and choices. Culminating in her experience at a Native American sweat lodge, Borella's book shows us that when we give up on normal, we can have relationships of true worth and sweetness.

A generous and thoughtful book that will appeal to anyone trying and failing to "be like everyone else."

Stephanie Barbé Hammer, author of *Journey to Merveilleux City* and *Pretend Plumber*

What young person has not wished to be normal, and accepted by other teens? Even as adolescents rebel in their music, clothing, and slang, they are in fact copying one another and donning a uniform and persona that is approved by their peers. Francesca Borella was no different in her striving to fit into her community and schools. But coming from a family marked by divorce, poverty, alcohol abuse, and even the involvement of Child Protective Services made "normal" an impossibility. So, as an adult, she dedicated herself to acquiring all the trappings of the American Dream—higher education, a nice home, and a traditional marriage and family. But life had other plans, and this honest memoir movingly chronicles Francesca's journey to accept and even celebrate the ways in which her life would never be ordinary.

Lynda Smith Hoggan, author of *Our Song: a Memoir of Love and Race*

The open spirit of Francesca Borella's voice matters in an historical moment when too many Americans justify terrible cruelty in the name of "normalcy." As mother to a trans child, Borella traces her own path to understanding as she explores her traumatic background, her struggles with relationships, her love for learning and discovery, and a deep longing to be free from the small-minded judgments of others.

Jo Scott-Coe, author of *Unheard Witness* (UT Press)

No Hope For Normal

Francesca Borella

CONTENTS

LIST OF PHOTOS

PROLOGUE

How do we know what is true? Memory is a tricky thing. I remember a very specific event in which we had tacos for dinner one night when I was a child. My older sister Ann ate seven tacos and ended up being very sick that night, throwing them all up. I spoke to my younger sister Donna about this memory, and she says she remembers the night, but Ann had eaten seven pork chops, not seven tacos. We both agree with the number seven, but the food is different. How could that be? I asked Ann, since the event focused on her, and to my surprise, she didn't remember it all. It's such a mystery, how our brains store memory. As I was writing this memoir, I thought about all these stories and events that I have included in my book and about how many people will probably argue with me later about what really happened. I have come to the position that we each experience the world through our own perceptions and realities. If you don't agree my story is true from your worldview, I can only say it is true to me. I changed a few names for privacy reasons.

NO HOPE FOR NORMAL

CHAPTER 1

John, still wearing his khaki field biology clothes, marched into the bedroom with that look on his bearded face that told me he wanted to talk about something I didn't want to talk about. He would always corner me when I was exhausted after teaching at the college all day and when I hoped I could grab a quick nap in the late afternoon, or early evening. He closed the door.

"I'm taking Ray to the transgender clinic in Los Angeles to get a prescription to start hormone therapy," he said.

I sat up. My heart started racing. "Why are you doing this?"

"I want to support my child, not alienate her," he said, first pacing one side of the room and then the other.

"She is only seventeen. Can't this wait until her brain is more mature?" I asked.

"The psychiatrist thinks this is important. Ray will be much happier if she can look more masculine. I don't like this either, but it's not going away. Rebecca is Ray now."

Tears welled up in my eyes and I couldn't see clearly. My stomach tightened, and I almost felt like I was going to throw up. I hated that my daughter had gender dysphoria and was turning into a male. About five years earlier, Rebecca started talking about feeling masculine. I had hoped it was a product of adolescent identity seeking, but her insistence that she was male became firmer when the psychological counseling and psychiatrist appointments began.

"Fine. Whatever. I hate this. It just makes me sick. All of this." I put my hands over my face to cover my eyes.

John was being the responsible one, going to all the medical appointments with Rebecca. I was avoiding it all. Because of that, there was so much stress in the house. I was worried about all the serious mental illness in John's family, like with his grandfather, uncle, and sisters. I thought, maybe Rebecca was starting to manifest bipolar disorder, schizophrenia, or something else. Rebecca was already taking medication for anxiety.

Then, there was talk about future breast surgery, a mastectomy. Rebecca already bound her breasts to look flat-chested. She also cut her hair. I was scared. I didn't want her to do any permanent body changes. I had visions of the little girl she used to be with her long, blond braids, the one who had loved to wear pink and purple clothes and play with her stuffed animal toys like they were her babies. Where did that little girl go? Almost every day, behind closed doors, John and I fought about all of this.

The stress from dealing with Rebecca was taking a heavy toll on our marriage. In the back of my mind, though, I knew we had survived other near-divorce, traumatic times together, so I was hopeful our relationship could endure. Although some days I felt like running away, I wasn't ready for that quite yet. John kept strong and I cried a lot.

"I just don't get it, Francesca," John said with his hand on his hip. He was pissed off. "You're educated and always the most understanding and accepting of people who are different. You're outspoken and supportive of gay, lesbian, and transgender rights at your school. But not when it's your own kid."

"I just want her to wait until she is mature," I said.

This was so frustrating. I didn't understand why I was so

resistant, either. My parents were very liberal about these ideas when I was growing up. I was taught to be accepting. My mom fought against the rigid gender lines of her time. She was a brilliant mathematician and wanted to be an engineer. In the 1950s, her options didn't include that. If she worked, she would most likely be a secretary, or she could not work and be a stay-at-home mom. At home, she was miserable, so I knew from her example to follow my desires.

That's why I became an anthropologist. It was my passion for diverse people that brought me to the field, despite all the discouragement. "You'll never get a job," was the most common comment I got when I told people I was studying anthropology. In this field, however, I learned even more about gender. I was surprised to find that in many places there are multiple, or alternative, gender roles. As a child, I had assumed there were only men and women. I thought about the third gender *Hijras* in India, the five genders in Navajo-Diné culture, and more. I knew, academically, our rigid, Euro-American gender lines had been breaking down for decades. There was a lot of dialogue about it on Tumblr and other social media. Now people were beginning to become who they really believed they were meant to be. My daughter must want the same thing.

I even thought about how working at Disneyland as a teenager in the 1970s had informed me. I worked seasonally in a restaurant, and after leaving for the summer and returning during Christmas vacation, my male boss had transitioned to a female. It was the first time I had ever met a transgendered person. At first, I was shocked. I didn't know people could do that. Ultimately, it didn't affect the working relationship between us. In no time, it seemed that she had never even been a man.

I thought deeply. Yes, I was okay with people being transgender. There had to be other reasons why I was freaking out about my kid becoming transgender. I just had to figure out what they were. I stewed over this situation every day, again and again.

Often, I would think, Why is this happening to me? It was as if Ray's transgender identity was an affront to my life. Even though I knew it was selfish to think this, I thought it wasn't fair. Maybe I subconsciously thought this was too weird? That word. Weird. I was used to it. I was always the weird one. Then it clicked: I was starting to figure it out.

All my life, all I ever wanted was normality. I dreamed of being normal because my life, thus far, had been anything but normal. I grew up in the age when television told us what normal life was supposed to be like. We saw it on TV in *Leave It to Beaver*, *Father Knows Best*, and *My Three Sons*, ideal family lives, having only occasional problems with kids breaking windows or not doing chores. On TV, the parents loved each other, didn't yell at their kids, and the home was neat and orderly with routine. I never had any sense of being normal, so far. I always had an unstable, unpredictable, screwed-up life. My parents divorced in the sixties, my mom was an alcoholic, and as a kid, I was physically awkward and far too skinny. My crazy upbringing left me with unhealed wounds. Every time John and I argued, I would flash back to my parents' fights, and my anxiety levels would skyrocket. It was almost as if I had post-traumatic stress disorder. It didn't take much to trigger the anxiety switch, and I would feel scared, defensive, and worried like I had when I was a kid.

I married John after two failed marriages. I had hoped with him that I finally had my chance for a normal life. I just wanted to be a normal married woman, have a normal kid with a husband who loved me and whom I loved. I wanted the normal American dream, to own a nice home, have a good job, and finally be happy, like on TV. That had all gone out the window now. In my head, normal families didn't have transgendered children.

LEARNING INSTABILITY

CHAPTER 2

My parents were all East Coast. I was born in Connecticut. My dad was an engineer at AMF (American Machine and Foundry) and got transferred to the West Coast. His job transfer happened when I was only three years old. Both my parents were born in New York. My mom was Protestant, of mixed ancestry, with deep roots in colonial and even Native America, and had close ties to her family. My dad was Catholic and born to Italian immigrants. I don't know the circumstances of their meeting, no one ever talked about it, but they both served in the Air Force in World War II. Their relationship was volatile; I remember them yelling and stomping off to other rooms often. Yet, they were also passionate. I remember them often kissing and embracing. In our first home in Goleta, California, we eventually unpacked our family of five children into a three-bedroom tract house. Later, my two brothers were born while we lived there. As I think about those years, I remember some scary times.

The glass shattered as it hit the floor from behind the locked door.

"I'm going to kill myself!" she shrieked from the bathroom.

"No, Mom, no! Please come out," I begged. My sisters, Ann, Carol and Suzy, cried, and we pounded on the door.

"Please, Mom, please, come out." I was shaking with terror; I didn't know what else to say. My six-year-old brain didn't really know what was happening, but my older sisters all had tears streaming down their faces too, so I knew this was serious. I was scared and felt it down to the weakness creeping into my bones.

My dad slammed the door on his way out of the house. He was gone. He was always leaving, just when we needed him to stay. Daddy was everything to me, and I loved how his strong arms made me feel safe, but I knew if he didn't leave, the fight would never end. This one had gone on for a long time, and now it was dark. It seemed like they were always yelling at each other. Now it was quiet. My body hurt, even though nothing had happened to me, and I began shaking like I was freezing cold, even though it was summer. I didn't know then that my shaking was a trauma response.

The lock rattled, paint chips fell off the peeling door as it opened, and I saw my mom standing there, like a rabbit who had escaped a predator with her sanctuary burrow behind her. She didn't look like my mom anymore. She was sobbing and heaving. Her face was tear streaked. I could see the deep lines and puffy eyes that she tried to hide with chalky makeup. We all ran to her, jumped on her, and clung to her like cats escaping up a tree. Her stiff body slowly let go, and she wrapped her arms around all of us. I began to feel better too. It was over for now.

Later in the night, I was lying wide awake in bed. I snuggled closer to my sister for security. The front door opened with its familiar squeak. It was my dad coming back home. My parents started talking, but I could barely hear their words. Then, I could clearly make out Dad saying, "You've got to stop drinking." They weren't yelling, at least, so I felt a little better and knew eventually I would fall asleep. So many times, it was the same thing, over and over, again.

A few nights later, watching TV with my sisters before we got shuffled off to bed, I started to feel uncomfortable, all twitchy. This was an early experience of anxiety. I didn't understand it. I felt like I had just stepped on an ant trail and ants were all climbing up my legs. Daddy hadn't come home yet, and Mom was mad, I could tell. There was that smell of rotten orange juice, and she kept repeating herself. She must have had her nasty drink again. I wished Daddy would come home, so I could jump up and hug him, and brush off the imaginary ants.

"Where's Daddy?" I heard Ann ask. "What's taking him so long today?"

"Who knows?" my mom answered in an annoyed way. "Who knows… you know what though… let's go look for him. Yeah, let's go look for him. Get the kids in the car." She reached for her keys and dropped them on the floor.

"But it's almost bedtime," Ann said.

"Don't argue with me," our mom said and picked up her pocketbook from the table.

Ann hesitated, and then all the kids at home were gathered up and sent to the car, a big, wood-paneled station wagon. My oldest sister, Suzy, was spending the night at a friend's house, so there was only the five of us. We climbed into the back with a blanket and tried to get comfortable. We were all confused and a little scared, since we didn't know where we were going, and this was not something we would normally do at night. As we drove off with Ann in the front seat, I could see her sitting straight as a tree and staring straight ahead, watching the road. I wondered if she was afraid like me. I saw my mom's eyes in the rear-view mirror. She had that crazy, I-don't-know-who-she-is look. We drove for a while, and I hoped it would end soon.

"Mom! You just turned the wrong way down a one-way street!" Ann yelled. Ann's scream scared the younger kids, and Donna and Bruce started bawling.

I didn't know what she meant, but I started shaking again. I then froze still. Was I going to die? Did my mom want to die? All I could think about was Mom in the bathroom, shrieking that she was going to kill herself. Carol looked white as a ghost. My mom seemed possessed and too calm for such a mistake.

"Turn there! Turn there!" Ann pointed and tried to grab the steering wheel. Through the front windshield, I could see headlights aimed right at us, and suddenly our car jerked and veered down a side street. Ann sighed in relief. Mom stared straight ahead.

"You knew that was a one-way street! Why did you drive the wrong way? What were you doing? For God's sake, take us home! Take us home!" Ann was panicking.

No answer from Mom. She was like a robot. She continued to drive, but to me she was not my mom anymore. I began to cry.

Finally, she spoke, but her words weren't comforting, "Be quiet, all of you! You're okay. Stop it now!"

I was relieved when I saw familiar things out the window, the tall pine trees that I played near, the pink house next door, and finally our own cracked driveway. We all jumped out of the car like there was a fire drill, and Ann ushered us off to bed. I couldn't sleep, even snuggled next to my sister. Later, from my back bedroom, I heard Daddy come home and restore order with his voice. Even then, I couldn't go to sleep. Somehow, I knew I was lucky I had survived another day. Shivering, I wondered, Will I be so lucky tomorrow?

Our family wasn't always in turmoil. We appeared typical when we went to church together as an orderly little army. My Catholic father insisted we were all baptized and that we attend mass weekly, even if he didn't go. We went on little outings like Sunday drives to Lake Cachuma in the rolling hills above Santa Barbara or to the Danish-themed tourist trap town of Solvang. Our big treat at the end was a bucket of butter cookies from Birkholm's Bakery. My dad loved the outdoors and would often take us on picnics. We went to places like Nojoqui Falls and stood next to them to get our picture taken. Being in nature always made me happy, too.

On one particular trip, my dad stopped the car on the San Marcos Pass and pointed to a big bird in the sky. "Do you see that, kids? That's a condor. Look at it carefully. There aren't very many left, and by the time you grow up, there won't be any more." He sighed. He knew they were on the verge of extinction.

I studied the soaring bird from the car window. Although I really didn't understand, I knew that my dad had stopped the car to show us, so it must have been very important. I tattooed the image on my brain. I wished I could be like that bird, so carefree even with its impending doom.

Nojoqui Falls excursion with my dad taking the photo, near Lake Cachuma in Santa Barbara County. Back L-R: Suzy and Ann. Front L-R: Carol, me, and Donna

My mother, Beverly Jean Robertson

REAL MEN CRY

CHAPTER 3

"I'm going to wear slacks to the baptism party," my mom told my dad defiantly.

"It's not proper. Why can't you just do what the other women do sometimes?"

"I get tired of wearing dresses all the time, and we will be in a garden."

My dad shook his head and smiled. He didn't really seem to mind.

My mom served in the Women's Army Air Corps (WAC) and later became part of the Women's Air Force (WAF) in and after World War II. She had been enrolled in MIT as a math major when the war broke out. Not many women went to college, let alone majored in math in the 1940s. She jumped at the opportunity to serve in the military. After her service, as a stay-at-home mom, she liked to work in the yard. She didn't let her small frame stop her. She was five foot six, but very thin. She would happily don her pedal pushers with sneakers and tied-in-the-front blouse along with a broad-rimmed sun hat to go outside at any time. In those days, when she wanted to plant shrubs, it was physically hard work. The nursery plants she bought were in metal pots, and my mom had to split them apart using hefty tin shears. She dug deep holes with shovels with the skill of a professional gardener. There were often new flowers to plant on the borders of the yard, and every day there were weeds to pull. I loved the yard, too. One time, I took a potato from the house and planted it in the back yard. At the end of summer, I dug up the baby potatoes under the soil and brought them in the house to show everyone. My mom was so surprised. I told her I wanted to be a farmer, and she told me that I could do anything I wanted in life. I can still hear her say, "Where there's a will, there's a way."

A family rumor has it that it was in the military where my mother met my father. He served in the Air Force and loved to fly. Planes were his passion. We had photos and models of planes all over the house. Although my father was an engineer, his real joy was teaching flying on the weekends. Occasionally, my father would cook dinner, not like the typical Italian man waiting for his wife to serve him. No one made spaghetti like him. The sauce would cook for hours, and it had the tangy aroma of Italian sausage and sweet tomatoes and spices that would fill up the entire house. It made our stomachs growl. My friends didn't have fathers who cooked or mothers who did yard work all day, and that made me feel a little weird. Regardless, I learned it all, to cook and garden with great love. All of us kids were encouraged to try new things. Traditional gender roles were often blurred at home.

However, my mom was stuck home with the kids all day, and each morning my dad would put on his suit, complete with his airplane cufflinks and tie tack, and leave at 6:00 am for his desk job. All the females in the house wore dresses with gloves when we went to church. We were taught to be "ladylike" when we sat in chairs, holding our knees together and crossing our legs at the ankles.

My father used every spare moment of the day to sneak away to our garage to build a small plane, a real people-holding one, not a model. His workbench was ordered and neat. He would line up the tools he would be using each day, the hammers, saws, screwdrivers, and sanders. He would carefully wipe them down and put them away when he was finished. There were angled pieces of wood and a reddish resin glue my dad would put sawdust in to fix the wood together. My six-foot-four dad was always stooped over the wooden bench with measuring tapes, saws, and sandpaper. As a six-year-old child, I was completely fascinated and mystified by this grand construction project. My father would put me to work nailing useless pieces of wood together using his precious tools. The hammers were heavy, and woodworking wasn't something a girl would normally want to do, but I was sure I was making a huge contribution and happy my dad let me "help." Even as a child, I sensed that I needed to be as meticulous as he was because this was the most important thing in the world to him. I had a special bond with my dad because I was the only one of my six siblings who helped. He would regularly look over at me and smile as we worked without talking.

One day, my mother called out to us, "Al, come in here, the funeral is on TV."

"I'll be in in a bit. I have this one part of the wing I need to finish." He went back to his hammering.

"You should see little John-John saluting. My God, this is heartbreaking," my mother yelled.

The sound of the funeral got louder, since my mom turned up the volume so my dad could hear what was happening. He ignored it all, and I stayed by his side.

"Daddy, why did someone kill President Kennedy?" I asked. I wondered what it would be like for Caroline and John-John to not have a dad anymore.

"Sometimes, bad things happen to good people," he answered and returned to his work. My father had been so happy there was finally a Catholic president. He respected Kennedy, and I didn't understand why he didn't want to see the funeral. When the news that Kennedy had been shot broke a few days earlier, I heard Daddy telling Mom how horrible this whole thing was, with a tremble in his voice. I had first heard about the assassination at school, though. I saw the cafeteria workers crying and heard them telling each other the shocking news. I didn't understand, but I knew it was important. I thought my dad should have been watching the funeral with Mom, but he went deeper into the darker part of the garage, holding tight to his hammer. He turned so his face was away from me. As the funeral mass continued, he turned again, and I glimpsed a tear almost falling from his eye in the dappled light. I knew he didn't want me to see. Men weren't supposed to cry.

My Father, Albert Mario Borella

Me at about age 4

ABANDONED BROKEN DOLLS

CHAPTER 4

It was raining, and I shivered. My sister Ann was rushing us off to bed, and I overheard her talking to Suzy.

"When will Daddy be leaving?" Ann asked quietly.

Suzy whispered back to her, "I'm not sure, but don't talk about it around the other kids."

"What will happen if they get the divorce?" Ann's voice quivered.

That was the first time I heard the word "divorce." I didn't know what it was, but I could tell that it meant things were going to change. I was afraid. What I didn't know was that my life would become even more chaotic.

My parents divorced at a time when it was unusual to do that. My father's Catholic faith, technically, didn't even allow it, but due to their fighting and misery, it was necessary. Even as a child, I could tell that my dad struggled with my mom's daily volatile outbursts. Whenever Mom drank, she would turn into a different person. She would repeat herself over and over. She would obsess about anything my dad did wrong:

"Why didn't you fix that hole in the fence?" she yelled one day. I knew my dad was working overtime at his job and barely had time to eat and sleep.

"You're never home, and I have to take care of all these kids."

She repeated that three times.

"You don't love your family."

"The garage is a holy mess. It needs to be cleaned up."

I realized I hadn't seen them hug or even speak friendly to each other in a long time.

Then, my dad's patience ran out. He left. I don't fully know what happened between them; my mom's drinking must have played a role. There was a long court battle, and my dad disappeared. My mom was so angry with my dad for leaving her; she wouldn't let us kids see him when he wanted to visit us. I cried at night because he wasn't there. I thought of him during the day and wondered if he thought of us. It was like he had died. I just wanted our family to be together again.

My mom had less money to function with and that had horrible consequences. We moved to a new, smaller home, we wore hand-me-down clothes, and we ate less.

"I'm tired of eating oatmeal all the time," I proclaimed, as if I was the only one it bothered.

"Well, if your father paid his child support, we could get something else to eat." My mother gritted her teeth. "He makes enough money. He's just doing this to make me mad."

My stomach didn't like being in the middle of this. I resented my dad for leaving and not remembering that we would suffer too. I wish I knew why he was doing this.

As a single parent in Goleta in the 1960s, my mom tried to support her seven children alone by working secretarial jobs to pay the bills. There was never enough money, and we would often eat oatmeal for dinner. I was starving all the time. Mom would dish out dinner in equal proportions, and we all waited in anticipation to claim a bite of leftovers on another sibling's bowl or plate. That almost never happened. We were not fussy eaters at all. We just wanted food.

I would see my mom sitting in the living room at night with her drink in her hand and her eyes glazed over. She didn't garden anymore; she didn't do much of anything except sit and drink when she got home from work. Somehow, despite this, her newly acquired typing skills sharpened, and she eventually managed to get a better-paying job for a state senator in Los Angeles. My mom had to leave us during the week while my older siblings, Suzy, who was seventeen, and Ann, who was fifteen, watched us. Mom would stay at a friend's apartment in Los Angeles, only returning home on the weekends.

At school in the fourth grade, one day I was called into the office. The office secretary walked into my classroom and handed the teacher a note. She told me to follow the secretary. Once I was in the office, there was an older woman talking to the principal. I saw my sister there, too. I could feel adrenaline pumping up my heart rate. I knew this wasn't going to be good. The principal told me to go with this gray-haired social worker who would take me and my other siblings to the local juvenile hall. The woman looked like a grandmother with a bun high on her head and spoke to us as if she didn't want us asking any questions. I held my sister's hand and sat quietly while my other siblings arrived at the office. I had no idea what was going on but guessed the cranky old lady who lived next door, who criticized us for being such a big family, had reported my mother to the authorities. The gray-haired social worker didn't allow me to go back to my class for my belongings.

"Where are we going? Will my mom be there?" I asked. I wondered what juvenile hall was and what it would be like.

She answered, just as I thought she would, “Don’t ask questions.” She motioned for us to get up.

We shuffled out to a big car and were loaded in the back seats. Staring out the car window, I wanted the comfort of the Mary Poppins book I had in my desk. I had found the book in the school library and would check it out, over and over again. The picture on the cover had the familiar nanny flying over London with her umbrella. The story inside, however, was my favorite and made me hopeful about having a normal family life. Mary Poppins had saved the Banks family, and I was hoping that kind of magic could happen for my family. I read from that book every day.

Once we arrived at our destination, they separated my brothers from my sisters and myself. That was shocking. Why did the boys and girls have to be apart? I was scared and started to cry when they made them leave. My brothers were both preschool age, and I wanted to protect them. Next, they had to issue clothes to us. Was I going to have to stay here forever? I felt sick and dizzy. An apathetic middle-aged female guard ordered us to follow her.

“Come with me,” she ordered in a harsh voice like Cruella de Vil. My mind flashed on the evil villains in the Disney movies I had seen. This was not going to end well, I knew it.

My sisters and I walked down the cold, concrete hall to the linen and uniform room, where the heavy door had a crossed-wire, glass window. I could see metal shelves inside with stacks of sheets, towels, and clothes. The sounds of our footsteps, the unlocking of the door, and every small sniffle we tried to hide echoed in the emptiness of the Lysol-scented hall.

I waited in line with Suzy, Carol, Ann, and Donna to get our supplies, too scared to move.

"Next one!" the lady bellowed.

I stepped up to her to receive my supplies.

"What size do you wear?" she asked.

"Eight," I squeaked out.

The guard turned and pulled shirts, pants, pajamas, and other clothes from the shelves.

"We don't have any more girls' underwear in your size. You'll just have to wear boys," she said matter-of-factly.

My face turned hot, and tears ran down my cheek. I didn't want to wear boys' underwear. This was too much. Where was my mom? Why were we here? I received the stack, and Donna was up next.

After we were all provisioned, they showed us to the dormitory rooms where we would sleep. At least my sisters would be nearby at night. We put away our things, and again we were ordered to follow the guard. It was mealtime.

We were taught like soldiers in the army; there was a rigid schedule to everything, and everyone had to obey. I had to learn the signals to go wash before meals and to wait at the table. Grace was led by the guard before I could eat, even though we never did anything like that at home. I could not leave the table until we had all finished. After dinner, I read from the few dog-eared books or played with the few broken toys the institution had.

I was drawn to the dollhouse. It had torn wallpaper in the tiny rooms. The furniture was sparse. It felt like home to me. I tried to fix it all up with scratch paper, making origami-like folded chairs and tables. I carefully dusted out the rooms and integrated my new furniture. The dolls were a mess, though. Some were missing arms, or legs, or had tangled hair. One of them reminded me of

Suzy. She was the most intact doll, and she wore a dingy, off-white cloth dress. Her hair was matted. I thought about how Suzy would tease her hair into a high bouffant. I made this doll take care of the others. I called her "the mom." The other two were more like Donna and me. They were smaller. They had broken limbs and no clothes; I covered their wounded bodies with paper gowns I had made for them. It still didn't seem like enough because I knew they were sad being scarred and incomplete. The mom doll nurtured them. I sat them all at the dining table with imaginary feasts. I had the mom tell them bedtime stories as she tucked them in for the night. With all that was wrong, I wanted them to have as good a life as they could.

Then, with another signal, I knew it was time to get ready for bed. I showered, brushed my teeth, and put on my pajamas. I slowly walked to the dormitory room and crawled between the cold sheets of the small metal bed. I missed sleeping in the same warm double bed at home with Carol and Donna.

When my mother finally came to visit, I jumped up and down. My little brothers, Bruce and Brian, were brought in with us. We all raced to Mom and clung on her body like leeches, hugging each other as well. I cried and begged to go home.

"We hate it here, Mom!" I said through my sobs.

"They are so mean about everything," Carol whimpered.

"It's cold and ugly," little Donna whined.

"Don't worry, you'll all be coming home soon," Mom assured us, with tears in her eyes. Then, too soon, just as we started to laugh together and play games, we were ordered to go back to the dormitory again. I cried for hours.

When I think back from my adult perspective at the traumatic institutional experience, my thoughts are unclear. I don't even remember how long we were there. It could have been weeks, but my sense of time was blurred since I have no memory of being outside in sunlight where I could see the days start or end. Eventually, we went home to my mom, who then moved us to the Los Angeles area.

My poor, exhausted, overworked mother had to endure yet another legal trial, where she had to prove she was not an unfit mother. Sexism in the 1960s did not allow her to work a job with a decent salary. I know she loved us, but she had become dependent on alcohol. Her daily drinking was getting worse. Her new job always had alcohol available at the political events she was required to attend. Eventually, she changed her job to one in which she transcribed court reporting. We got to see her a lot more, since she did most of her typing at home. That really wasn't much better. She was distant and tired all the time, slurring angry curses at my father, rewriting her memories with a bottle before passing out in the early evenings, reeking of her vodka. Half-awake in the middle of the night and early dawn, I'd hear her typing. The constant tap-tap-tapping drone of the typewriter, a new-style electric one, became the white noise we all slept through. She would type just enough of her transcripts to earn enough money to keep us going, but not enough to pay all the bills. Sometimes the electricity would get turned off for a day or two, sometimes the gas bill wasn't paid so we had to take baths in cold water and barbecue our hot dog dinner. We rarely had a working phone in the house. She had other bills, too, because bill collectors were looking for her. When they figured out where we lived and started pounding on the door, we moved. We never stayed in a house for longer than a year. We would wake up one day, and my mom would tell us we were moving that day. Just like that, we were gone. I didn't get to tell my friends at school goodbye. After a few moves, I stopped making friends; it just wasn't worth the effort, knowing we would be moving again.

At that time, I never knew anyone who had divorced parents and who lived with a single mom. I never knew anyone who had a parent who drank too much. I never knew anyone who had been in juvenile hall. These events added to my low self-esteem as junior high approached. I felt ashamed and embarrassed by my family. With my awkward emerging adolescent body, I just knew that I was going to be too tall and too thin. My sense of shame increased.

SEEKING SELF-ESTEEM

CHAPTER 5

Just before I went to junior high school, my mother remarried. Our new stepfather was a used car salesman named Bob, who looked exactly like President Lyndon B. Johnson: old, wrinkled skin, and thin, balding hair, except Bob wore wire-framed glasses. I'm not sure what my mom saw in him, except that she must have been looking for some financial help. What motivated Bob, though, is a mystery. Although my mom was attractive, I can't imagine why this guy would marry her with seven dependent children. When he moved in, he seemed nice enough. He quickly learned our names and tried to engage us in conversation. We quickly learned that he smoked and even cursed, both behaviors we had never experienced before by someone in the home. Regardless, we were all hopeful that he would treat us like we were his own kids, like a real dad.

We moved to a typical Southern California suburban rental house in Simi Valley. There were four bedrooms and lucky for us, a built-in swimming pool. Even though I was about to enter adolescence, it was the first time I had ever seen one of those. I couldn't swim. None of my six siblings, except Suzy, who had learned in high school, knew how to swim. The house was roomy, and the pool looked like it could be a lot of fun. After we experienced several moves and plenty of disruptions in our lives, this new place looked like a home. I didn't want to move anymore.

Bob and Suzy decided we needed swimming lessons. "Are you

ready?" said Bob out of the side of his mouth where there wasn't a cigarette burning. He grabbed my arm and tossed me into the deep end. Suzy was there in the water to catch me and help me get to the side. One by one, my siblings made their splash, dog-paddled to side, and laughed as they climbed out. We weren't scared at all because we really wanted to swim. "Do it again!" we squealed. Within no time, we were all swimming like pros.

For the first time, I made friends easily because when you have the only pool in the neighborhood in a hot Southern California summer, you have a magnet to draw in friends. All my new friends loved to swim, too. For three years, especially in the summer, we were in the pool at every opportunity. By the end of a pool day, our vision would be blurry from the chlorine and the hours we'd spent underwater seeking toy pearls we'd thrown in, all the while pretending we were mermaids. The water was a fantasyland, a playground full of fun with lots of laughter. Our sun-cooked bodies were chocolate brown, accented by the golden streaks in our bleached-out hair. I grew tall and skinny and hit my adolescent years, ready for junior high school.

When I got to junior high, I didn't make any friends there. My neighborhood friends were mostly younger than me and still at the elementary school. Besides, when I was away from the pool at school, I didn't have what other kids valued. I was shy and, physically, I looked odd. I was too skinny, having grown a foot taller in one year. I was five-foot-eight and only weighed one hundred pounds. The kids at school teased me. "You look like a refugee." One girl snarled, "Doesn't your mom feed you?" "Francesca Gorilla! Francesca Gorilla!" a boy teased. "Hey Lanky, is your real name String Bean?" another girl said. "Skinny Bones Jones!" They would laugh together.

Their taunts were relentless. I hung my head low and ate my lunch alone every day. After school, though, if the weather was nice, I went straight into the pool. The water embraced me, and I glided effortlessly and gracefully in my happy aquatic domain.

One day Mom came to us and announced, "I think you kids need some riding lessons." My mother thought some kind of formal lessons would be good for us. She wanted us all to have horseback riding lessons because my other sisters were fanatics about horses, and horseback riding would mix us with a different class of people. My mom thought we could learn some social skills and values that would serve us well in the future. By paying a reasonable monthly fee, discounted because there were multiple siblings, we could use the stable's horses and feel like we were more than poor people. I wasn't crazy about the idea, but I loved animals.

During one lesson, my horse for the day was feisty. We entered the area, and the teacher called out the tasks to perform. "Walk your horses." Then, "trot your horses" and "cantor your horses." At that point, my horse knew I was not in control and took off running away with me, out of the arena and up a hill. I hung on for dear life while the trainers galloped out to save me. I didn't like that horse, and I didn't want to ride anymore. My mother just shook her head. "What are we going to do with you?" I knew what I wanted. "Just let me take dancing lessons, please?" I begged.

I dreamed I would be a musical movie star. If my mom wanted some upward mobility for us, being a famous actress would fit the bill. I wanted to be like Ginger Rogers in the old musical movies. I loved watching her in *Swing Time* with Fred Astaire. She was so light-footed and graceful. Swimming in the pool made me realize that I could be graceful. I knew how to remember things easily, too. Without too much persuading, my mom agreed to dancing lessons. It turned out that I was fairly talented with dance. I was coordinated and I learned quickly. I loved to move with the music, just like I moved in the pool. I found a way to feel beautiful, despite the ongoing teasing at school. I even organized little dance classes in my garage for my neighborhood friends. Dancing made me happy and hopeful about my future. After only a few months of lessons, as money became tight, my classes ended. The upcoming seasonal dance show required costumes. How I longed to wear the hot pink and orange mini dress with go-go boots, as we performed our dance to the song "Thoroughly Modern Millie." We were too poor to afford the costumes. Heartbroken, I wished I was one of the normal kids at the dance class who had moms cheering them on and hand sewing all their costumes. It didn't really matter in the end; we would be moving to a new home and would have ultimately missed the show.

Our family in Simi Valley after my mom married my stepfather when we learned to swim. Back L-R: Carol, Ann, Suzy, and Mom. Front L-R: me, Brian, Bruce, and Donna (between Mom and Bruce)

I FEEL THE EARTH MOVE

CHAPTER 6

My stepfather became a truck driver and that meant we had to move. Our new home was in Agoura Hills. We didn't have a swimming pool, but my emerging optimism led me to believe that my life would get happier. Things might begin to turn around, I hoped, as being a slender teenager who was now also developing small breasts might work to my advantage. I wasn't getting any taller, and soon I would have a stable adult body. I longed for a stable life, not changing physically, staying in one place, safe and secure. I was tired of the new and unknown.

It started with a low hum and grew louder, glasses clanging, shattering crashes and unidentifiable thumps from every direction. In the din, I heard my mom screaming, "Get out of here. Move, move!"

I saw her tumble down the long hall, from one bedroom to the next. The floor over a concrete foundation rolled up and down like a snake slithering across the ground. "Whoa, far out. It's an earthquake!" I said sarcastically. My little sister, Donna, lying in the bed next to me, was freaked out and started crying. My smug teenage attitude would have to wait.

I grabbed Donna's hand, and we wobbled out, bumping the hall walls on one side, then the other. Out the front door, in the early morning light, we saw houses across the street wavering like folded origami in the wind. We collapsed on the dew-covered lawn, wearing only our thin cotton nighties. A fountain from a broken pipe sprang up by the undulating driveway, and our misted bodies shivered.

My younger brothers, Bruce and Brian, staggered out the front door. The older siblings, Carol and Ann, and finally, Mom emerged and stumbled toward us with arms full of blankets.

The shaking stopped.

"Mommy, mommy," Brian wailed. I could smell that he had wet his pants. We wrapped our bodies in the warmth of the blankets and Mom's embrace, but we continued to tremble.

The 6.7 Sylmar earthquake had lasted only a minute. It was the first earthquake I felt. I learned that even our solid ground, firm and strong most of the time, is not stable. Earthquakes are a regular phenomenon in Southern California, and I would experience many more, many smaller ones, and even a few bigger ones, through the years. This instability became normal for me. It didn't bother me. Everything else in my life was unstable, and like the earthquakes, I was used to it.

A RAT, A GUITAR, AND A DECK OF CARDS

CHAPTER 7

As I stood by the car, the slate sky looked like it was late evening in the Santa Monica Mountains. It was only noon. The sun behind the smoke was a faint orange ball. Ashes drove into me like snow in a blizzard. The gusts from the scorching Santa Ana winds almost pushed me over. My eyes stung and I could hardly breathe. I held a washcloth over my mouth and nose, trying to filter out some of the smoke. I saw my mom coming out of the house, leading my brothers behind her. "Are you ready?" she yelled. "The fire has spread all the way to Malibu Beach. It's official. We've been ordered to evacuate." My stepfather, Bob, was driving a long-distance route and would not be home for days.

I had already grabbed my pet rat and my guitar from my room: "Yeah. I have what I need." I inched my way to the other side of the car. I had been ready to go for the last ten minutes or so. I thought about how Malibu Canyon would be blackened and barren and look like a moonscape. Every spring, the canyon teemed with wildflowers, especially lupines. I thought of the feeling of walking through the waist-high flowers. They smelled sweet, a little like honey suckle but still unlike anything else. I always felt such joy looking out on the oak trees there and the occasional rabbits hopping nearby. I loved these mountains with all their beauty and wildlife, and I hiked them regularly with my high-school classmates. But now, my heart was racing, my body felt like lead, and the contents of my stomach rolled.

My three sisters came out of the house carrying bags overflowing with clothes and blankets. My mom opened up the car and everyone tried to get in at once. Normally, everyone would yell and talk at the same time in our family. No one spoke.

After my mom pulled out of the driveway, fire engines came toward us, and I wondered if this was the last time I would see our house before it burned down. Thoughts of what I would lose, like my books and my clothes, my record player and my albums, swarmed in my head. I saw visions of the paintings on the living room walls, the couches and the television, and I brushed them off. No big deal. Then I thought of the rose bushes, the chrysanthemums, and the wild rabbits that had fled to our yard. What would the poor rabbits do when the fire approached?

Slowly, we inched past the sheriffs and fire trucks that now lined our street. The firemen in lemon yellow got out and dragged hoses toward the flames. We left our neighborhood and headed to the shelter, past the tract of houses to Malibu Canyon Road. The fire was on both sides of the road, and we saw a eucalyptus ignite like a giant Fourth of July sparkler. As we drove under the tree, the flames were hot through the glass of the car window. I thought that this must be what hell's like. Crimson embers fell from the sky like glitter.

Still, no one spoke, and my mom drove on.

The evacuation center was at Arthur E. Wright Middle School; Mom parked, and we waited. We listened to the radio in the car. The wind was dying down, and the sounds became clearer. The news reporters talked about the number of acres that had burned, from the mountains to the sea, and the direction the flames were heading. They interviewed residents in the fire zone, the fire captains, and the sheriffs. I didn't hear anything about our neighborhood and worried if it had burned.

"I need to go to bathroom—bad," my brother announced.

Mom told us to leave our stuff and come back for it if we needed it. We spilled out of the car and followed her to the gym. We were welcomed by Red Cross volunteers, and my mom pointed to the bathrooms. We all ran.

After having just driven through a fire vortex, tormented by the images of all our material life going up in flames, my siblings spent three hours playing crazy eights and drawing flowers. I played my guitar while trying to hide my rat under my shirt. My mom just stared off into space. Before we knew it, we got word that we could go back home. Mom snapped out of it when we were assured that none of the houses in our neighborhood were lost. Quickly, like an organized army, we filed back into the car and drove off.

Now we could see the hills that the smoke had hidden earlier, and everything on them was gone, melted into blackness. The hills seemed bigger, and small pillars of smoke rose from a few places where trees had once stood. When we arrived home, the fire engines were still parked on the road and some firefighters were resting on our lawn. Their dingy yellow clothes were smudged with ash and soot. Their eyes were outlined, like raccoons, from the goggles they had removed. We waved to them as we climbed out of the car. Too tired to lift their hands, they barely smiled back at us.

My mom whispered to me, "Go help Ann make some sandwiches to give these guys." I ran into the house. The smell of smoke was everywhere, even inside. I wondered if it would always reek like this.

Ten sandwiches later, we distributed them to the exhausted, hungry men with our gratitude for their hard work and for saving our home. Even as a teenager, I knew that fires in Southern California were common and that there would be more in my future. I never reconciled with these abrupt and unsettling moments of loss. Nothing for me is ever safe and secure.

SHINE

CHAPTER 8

In my freshman year, I decided I had to do something that would set me apart from the others. I was tired of being in the background of the teenage world. Middle school was dreadful, with few friends, and I was determined to change that. What could I do though? I knew girls in the pep squad got chosen by being popular already, or they were beautiful with perfect curvy bodies and large breasts. I was a skinny, small-breasted nobody. However, I adopted my mother's mantra: "Where there's a will, there's a way."

When I tried out to be a baton twirler, a majorette for Agoura High School, it wasn't a normal situation. I really didn't know what I was doing, and I certainly had never been taught to twirl properly with lessons of any kind. On the day of the audition, since I had learned a few moves, I faked it, a lot. I wanted the title of majorette badly. I wanted to be someone; a cheerleader, a song leader, a band member, anything. I wanted to wear a sparkly blue-and-gold uniform and participate in the pep rallies. I sought to be popular, and I had to perform one of those roles. Being popular became my quest because the number of friends I attained would give me status. I was also boy crazy, and I knew that being on pep squad would get me noticed by boys. What I had going for me that day was that those selecting who would be a majorette were less knowledgeable about twirling than me.

Watching the Rose Parade on New Year's Day had given me

the idea. It was like seeing a beacon shining in the fog directly on the answer: the majorettes. The majorettes were always in front of the bands. They were the leaders, twirling and throwing their magical shiny batons high in the sky as they pranced in their brilliant sequined bodysuits in front of the high school marching bands. I wanted that. I wanted to be able to do something that required talent. I wanted to dress in a flashy way. I wanted to be a leader. I hadn't seen any majorettes at our school, so I wasn't even sure if that was a possibility. Also, I would need to learn to twirl a baton. However, I wouldn't dwell on all that, and I got right to work. Because I had gone through dancing lessons a few years earlier, I knew some jazzy moves, sashays, and striking poses, and after lots of practice with a broom handle, I knew I could pretend to be a good twirler.

The first day of class after Christmas break, in P.E., I saw the pep squad coordinator, Miss Jones, and got my courage up to ask about tryouts: "Excuse me, Miss Jones, when will you be holding the auditions for next year's pep squad?" I didn't want to sound too eager, but the words just jumped out.

"We hold tryouts in April. It's still a few months away. Do you think you will try out?" she snarled, looking me up and down.

"Oh, I am a baton twirler, and I was hoping to try out for majorette," I replied, wanting to convince myself I was indeed a twirler. "The band really needs a majorette out in front for parades, and honestly, they should perform at half-time shows and pep rallies, too." I knew I had to sell myself. "For school spirit, right?"

"We haven't had anyone want to do that for a long time. I guess you could try out." Although I sensed her disapproval, I didn't care. I was so excited. I interpreted Miss Jones's words as if I had already been chosen. I ran quickly to tell my friends.

Several of my friends gathered as I danced around. "I'm going to try out for majorette!" I could hardly contain myself.

Then Susan spoke, "Oh! I should too! I took lessons in elementary school."

Oh no, I thought. I wasn't too thrilled to hear that because I didn't want any real competition. I loved Susan, and I didn't want to discourage my friend, so maybe we could work something out.

"Hey Susan, I have an idea. Why don't we practice twirling together after school? We can come up with a routine or something," I suggested, realizing she could teach me some real moves.

"Great idea," said Susan. She was always one to go along with my plans.

The next day after school and regularly until auditions, with batons in hand, we met up. My newly acquired silver metal baton felt thinner and stronger in my hands compared to the wooden dowel I had been using. I had earned money through babysitting and purchased this jewel. It made me feel like an authentic majorette. With this baton, I would succeed. Both Susan and I worked hard at a majorette dance routine. Susan taught me all she knew about twirling, and I taught her all I knew about dance. With what I thought of as my better sense of timing and movement, I believed I had gotten better than her in no time. I felt confident. I could twirl the baton through my fingers. I could twirl it in front of me, behind me, go around my waist, and even catch some throws. I was realistic enough to know that I wasn't ready for the Rose Parade, but I felt like I could fake it for the Agoura High School tryouts.

Finally, audition day arrived. When we signed in, there was another name under the majorette list: Laurie. Who was Laurie?

No one I knew could tell me anything. She wasn't in our circle of friends, and I started to panic. I didn't expect any more competition; I mean no one had tried out for years. What if she was a good twirler? I tried not to let the possibility freak me out. They were calling for us, and I had to keep my cool. Then, there was another psychological blow. We were asked to do our routines individually. Susan got up to perform first in her frumpy, oversized gym clothes. She did well, but she was off beat to the music, as usual. I loved Susan, but I felt I had far more talent. Then it was my turn, and I too wore my equally ugly one-piece gym outfit. I hoped to perform my routine so flawlessly that my outfit wouldn't be noticed. I focused on my dance moves, smiling and posing with confidence. When I finished, I felt like I had performed like a Rose Parade star, the routine done absolutely perfectly.

Then Laurie was up. I had never seen her before. She was petite with hair that was slick and styled in a fancy bun. She wore too much makeup, and her fluffy skirt and skimpy shirt made her outfit fit skintight and looked Barbie-doll adorable. Ugh. I always hated it when people were naturally adorable. Most disturbing to me, though, was the fact that she wore majorette boots, with little gold tassels in front. She must be a real majorette with those boots. I wanted boots like that. The music started and she began. I focused on her twirling routine without missing a second of it. I watched to critique everything in detail, like a predator spying on prey. Her performance was good, I thought, but not better than mine. She was poised, but I thought to myself that her skill was only so-so, fancy boots and all. So, who would they pick?

That night I couldn't sleep. I felt like my entire social career in high school would be determined by the outcome. If I got this role, I could be popular and not feel like the loser I felt like I was in junior high. I couldn't bear to think about being like that again. Luckily, the results of the tryouts were posted the next day. We all gathered around the typed list as it was taped to the brick gym wall. There it was, my name. To my amazement, the other names were there, too. They had chosen all three of us to be a majorette team. Susan and I were so happy, we squealed and hugged, but Laurie didn't look happy. She put her nose up in the air and pranced off, saying "I'm the only one who really knows what they're doing!" We laughed and thought that she was probably right.

Fortunately, we were all sent to twirling camp in the summer and I got my first formal majorette training. I learned marching, spins, kicks and how to do the splits. For me, it was easy and fun. The team eventually learned to get along and we even added two more members the following year. Although we were never champions, we won some second-place awards in a few parade competitions. More importantly, once I became a majorette, people noticed me on campus.

"You're that majorette! I've seen you at the football half-time shows, right?" The boy looked older, taller, and very good-looking. Whoa. Was he speaking to me? He wasn't the kind of guy who would normally talk to me. My plan of becoming popular might have been working.

"Yeah, what do you think of our routine?" I replied. He was totally out of my league as an upper classman. "You chicks are hot!" he winked.

It felt good getting attention and I didn't want the conversation to end. I realized I had seen him before. "Hey, aren't you in the same math class as me?"

He patted the seat next to him to indicate that I should join him for lunch. "Yeah, can you help me with this homework? I noticed you're pretty smart, and I don't get what we're supposed to do."

Soon, it seemed that everyone on campus knew who I was. I didn't have to walk around being bullied and bent over in shame. Even if I wasn't the most popular girl in school, the boys started to pay attention to me. This was what I really wanted. I felt beautiful and feminine, and not too skinny and awkward. I didn't know it then, but I think the importance of having attention from boys helped fill the void of not having the father I loved around. It had been years since I'd seen him. My scheme to become a majorette worked out, just like I had planned when I watched the Rose Parade. I walked taller and smiled a lot more.

Learning to twirl the baton.

Our Agoura High School majorette team. Front to back: me, Laurie, and Susan

Me in majorette uniform for Agoura High School

DREAMER

CHAPTER 9

In high school I thought I wanted to be an actor. It was because many of my classmates had ties to the acting world in both movies and TV. Agoura was a haven just outside of Hollywood and Los Angeles and child actors, or children of actors and directors, went to my school. I could see that there were certain requirements for success that would make all aspiration difficult. I didn't have a rich financial background like my friends, or even family support cheering me on, but maybe I could still make it happen. I was never short on dreams. Sometimes I thought I was lucky, like when I got picked as a majorette. Possibly, my friendships could lead to opportunities, not something everyday people had a chance to do. In these times, not being a normal person might be okay. I needed acting lessons. I signed up for next semester's theatre class.

When I walked into the theatre class and met the teacher, Mr. Gilchrist, I didn't know what to expect. He was not an ordinary teacher. Mr. G, as we affectionately called him, reminded me of someone from the beatnik era. He was thin and always wore black, long-sleeved turtlenecks. His movements were exaggerated, and his lanky arms waved as he punctuated his voice with gestures. His pronunciation was clear and crisp, as if reciting a Shakespearean monologue. His eyes were wide open behind the thin, wire-framed glasses he wore. We were mesmerized by his daily performance and fully engaged by it, in a way we were not in any other class. Never have I ever met someone who loved the theatre more than he did. It looked like this man would help me and the other students learn what was needed to perform and create spectacular school drama productions. Every day, at the beginning of class, we were quizzed about playwrights and their works, from the Greeks to contemporaries:

"Name a play by Euripides!"

"Name of a Greek comedy writer?"

"Play by Christopher Marlow?"

"Who wrote *The Rhinoceros*?"

We loved this daily ritual and would shout out answers.

He would reward us, like a true actor, with, "Bravo! Bravo!"

We were taught to improvise, emote, and thrive on the stage. "Today, half of you will be household appliances and the other half will be cleaning the house!" We laughed and then transformed ourselves in our daily performances. The class was filled with aspiring actors and actresses. With so many classmates having family members in the movie business, we had no doubt that some would succeed. The truth was, though, that Mr. G wasn't interested in film. He loved the theatre.

"We are going to have tryouts for the next school play starting next Thursday. The play is *The Taming of the Shrew*!" He rolled the "r" and elongated the "ew." "Ah yes! What is more charming and entertaining than a play by the great William Shakespeare?"

"Ah yes," said George, a second-year acting student.

"I can hardly wait," said Kim. "I want to play Kate."

"Oh!" and "Yes," came from all the rest of us. I personally didn't know anything about the story and the only Shakespearean play I had ever seen was *Romeo and Juliet*. Even so, Mr. G's enthusiasm was infectious, and I knew it would be wonderful!

We all left school that day and immediately went to the library, our bookshelves, and the local bookstores to get a copy of *The Taming of the Shrew*. We read to each other and practiced the parts we dreamed to play. Everything about auditioning for a play was new to me since I had just started in drama class.

This play was about gender roles, how Kate was forcibly trained to abide in the appropriate female role, being a submissive wife. With the rising tide of feminism in the 1970s all around me, we were learning to be strong females. The play bothered me. I hated to read how Petruchio would withhold Kate's food and necessities to break her into submission and compliance. I yelled out loud in the quiet of my room, "Run away, Kate, this is ridiculous!" It occurred to me that this "normal" female gender role must have existed long before Shakespearean times. Did I really want to be part of reinforcing stereotypical gender roles that were starting to be broken down? I was confused by the play. I wanted to be a normal girl, but I didn't want to be normal like *that*. Of course, I wanted to be treated equal with men, with a voice and with control over my own life. It occurred to me that maybe this really wasn't what the play was about. Maybe it was just a satire on what not to do between men and women. I didn't understand.

I thought there was great talent in our class, beyond what I believed I possessed. I knew my classmates would all be trying out for the play. My self-esteem was on the mend after being a majorette, but it still had not completely recovered from the junior high school days. I rationalized that many of my classmates were upper classmen and had been around acting their whole lives, so they were more suited to be in the play because of their experience. I didn't think I had any chance to score a part at all. Also, I was just beginning my first drama class. I chickened out. I decided not to audition.

I had to think of a way to be involved, though. Finally, I figured out where I could be of help. I could offer my advanced sewing skills and work on the costume crew. It was a great way to participate in the play and see the behind-the-scenes activities that would take place.

After tryouts, the cast was chosen, the technical crews were lined up and the rehearsals began. My decision to work on the costume crew was a good one. I saw enormous talent in George and Kim reading their lines, and in their portrayals of Petruchio and Kate. It sent goosebumps over my body. How I wished I could have their talent. My admiration for Mr. G's patience and passion increased as I observed the daily practice runs transform into a polished play. That was something I could emulate.

Years later, when I became a professor, I always kept a vision of his teaching approach with me. I loved his respect for the students, hands-on activities, and the tons of enthusiasm that he had. In my mind, this formula allowed me to gain the same rapport with my own students when I began teaching. Even though most of my students will not all end up in my field as anthropologists, I hope to fill them with the enthusiasm for learning that Mr. G. had given to me. Even when, ultimately, I decided not to go into acting.

A NIGHT TO REMEMBER

CHAPTER 10

"Hey Francesca! Hey Francesca! Want to go to the Emmy Awards?"

Lori came charging up to me, waving her hands as I sat on my front lawn. She was my best friend in high school because she lived in my neighborhood. We would hang out together after school and on weekends.

"How could we do that?" I yelled back, wondering what she had in mind for this feat.

Lori and I were always scheming to become famous. I loved that about her. Although she was a rare down-to-earth girl in Agoura, probably because her mom grew up on a farm in the Midwest, she dreamed like me. In one plan, we would become rock stars. We formed a band called the Malibu Surf Finks. I strummed three chords on the guitar, and she drummed on a small plastic trash can turned upside down. We didn't let our lack of musical talent deter us, though. Living in this town, we had plenty of acquaintances, or knew of their family members, involved in acting or some other aspect of the movie industry to keep us motivated. Because of those connections, we sometimes got to be extras in movies. Lori's father was even a film editor, and a good one. Sometimes famous people would come to her house to consult with her dad about a project. I liked that even though her dad had won many awards for his skill, including Oscars and

Emmy Awards, Lori wasn't snobby like most movie people.

By the time Lori got to me, she could hardly stand still. "My dad has three tickets to the Emmys, and he can't go. He said we could use them if we can get there."

I grinned. I felt a jolt of adrenaline and I thought this could be great. I was thinking, This was just the opportunity we needed. Going to the Emmy Awards was a great prospect because someone would discover us there and beg us to be in their TV show. There was a problem though; neither Lori nor I knew how to drive, even though we were both old enough. We didn't have access to a car, either. I sat for a minute and wondered how we could do this. Maybe we could find someone to go with us who knew how to drive and had a vehicle.

"Far out! I'm in, but we need a driver. Hmm, what about Jen?" I asked. "I bet she'd go if we asked her."

"That's a great idea! Ask her tomorrow. I gotta go now. I'll call you later." With that, she turned, ran, and jumped in the open door of her mom's car, which was inching back and out of their driveway.

Jen lived in the housing development in the next canyon. We would often hike over the hills to hang out with her on weekends. She lived with her sister and her lonely dad. He didn't like to spend money, and so to save a few bucks and keep himself busy, he would tinker with old cars and keep a few junkers running. Jen drove one of his old trucks, from the fifties, a Chevy, dented and spray painted with primer in a few places which gave it a camouflaged appearance. She only used it when she needed to drive to the store or do other errands because it was a challenge to drive with a "three on the tree" stick shift on the steering column and an engine that ran rough and regularly stalled.

Most of the time, like when she would visit our neighborhood, she thought it was easier to run from place to place. In the hilly area around Agoura, nothing was nearby. Jen could run twenty miles in a day, from canyon to canyon. In fact, she was so good at running, she became the first girl on the varsity cross-country team. We were all a little jealous of her, but she was sweet. What made her endearing to us was her ceaseless sense of humor and her shrill laugh. Her laugh was unique and just hearing it made us laugh. We always had a great time with Jen. Going with her to the Emmys would be a blast.

The next day at school I could hardly wait to find her. At lunch time, I saw her sitting at a table by herself. I thought it was the perfect opportunity to ask, so other friends wouldn't get jealous. I casually sat down next to her on the cold metal bench. "Hey Jen. How's it going? I was just wondering, did you ever want to go to Hollywood and hang out with the stars?"

"Ha! That's a weird question." She bit into her apple.

"Lori's dad said we could use his tickets to go to the Emmy Awards." I smiled. "Of course, you were the first person we thought of who might want to go with us." A bigger smile was on my face now. "Jen, it could be so fun. Just us girls. And, honestly, we need a ride. It's on May 20th."

She swallowed her bite. "I'll probably have a meet that day."

My heart sank. If Jen didn't come, we couldn't go. The cross-country coach, Mr. Johnson, went walking by as we both looked up. "Jen! Quick. Go ask Mr. Johnson."

Jen leapt off the bench and sprinted over to Mr. Johnson, who was far enough away that I couldn't hear a word. As they talked, I watched for any clues as to what they were saying. Jen looked back at me and smiled. Just as quickly, she sprinted back.

"It's okay! There's no meet that day, or for several days after that. Hey, remember, I only have that old clunker of a truck. It stalls all the time, it's missing a fender, and it eats up gas like there's no tomorrow."

"Yeah, and it can get us to Hollywood. I'm so excited!" I squealed.

"Don't we have to dress up and look good? I don't have any clothes like that."

"Don't worry, we can fix you up! We'll beg, borrow, or steal what we need to be the most glamorous girls there!"

Jen looked at her legs. "Yeah, I'll look like Minnie Pearl on Hee Haw. You guys will have to help with gas money."

"Out of sight! I just love you, Jen!"

Weeks passed and we planned, schemed, and saved money. We fasted to save our lunch money, cashed in soda bottles we collected, and did ironing and babysitting for neighbors. On the night of the Emmys, using ancient prom dresses that were donated by my older sisters and their friends, we were made up and decked out like ball debutantes at our coming-of-age celebration. These dresses might not have been in style, but it was a funky time in the seventies. We could get away with more if we acted like we knew what we were doing. We decided to add some turquoise jewelry and shawls to look more sophisticated. Truly, I felt ultra-feminine and gorgeous in my floor-length, pink linen, A-line shift. I pinned my hair up in a coiffed French twist, which made me look older. Jen was all frilly in a peasant dress, with her wavy, red hair hanging long and hippy-like. She looked like she was heading to the Renaissance Faire, not a Hollywood event. Lori looked the part more. She wore a chic, silky blue gown and curled her slick black hair. To us, she looked like Elizabeth Taylor.

At last, we were ready, and even though we were worried about what others would think, we strutted out to the truck, exuding imagined elegance.

With a sputtering engine and smoke bellowing out the exhaust pipe, we chugged though the Valley on the 101 freeway. We arrived in Hollywood and drove up to the theatre where the red carpet was spread. All the eyes of the stars' fans who lined the sidewalk turned to see who the crazy party crashers were, sticking out like a sore thumb in the line of limousines waiting to unload their famous cargos. A valet ran up to Jen's window and started yelling.

"I'm sorry. I'm sorry. You must leave this area. This is the entrance to the Emmy Award Ceremony. Go turn around over there!" He pointed to an empty parking place.

"C'est d'accord. Ne vous inquiétez pas, nous sommes actrices vont à la cérémonie. Voici nos billets," I said in the best French accent I could muster, waving the ticket in front of him. Finally, I could put my French class lessons to the test. Also, I figured we needed to be foreign visitors to avoid arguments. We laughed and pretended we didn't understand anything else as he continued to mutter. At last, he sighed and smirked and walked away, shaking his head. Maybe he was on to us, but he let us continue.

We pulled up to the red carpet and disembarked. The next valet responsible for parking cars sneered as Jen handed him the truck keys. Everyone on the sidewalk watched us, snickered, and whispered to each other. We could hear people asking who we were to the photographers and reporters who were snapping photos and scribbling notes. We started to giggle and shake a little.

"Oh man. Take a deep breath. Let's go," I whispered. "Be confident!"

With our heads held high, we walked the carpet into the ceremony like we were the greatest movie stars that ever lived. We smiled, waved, and waited for the host. No one interviewed us, no one waved to us, and finally, we were ushered off to a table in the far back of the room. No one gave us another look all evening. That was their loss, we thought. We would have fun anyway.

We saw Richard Thomas, the actor who played the innocent, well-behaved John-Boy from *The Waltons*, tipsy and angry, talking to one of his friends about having been in a fender bender on the way to the presentation. We would never have thought that the actor playing such a goody-boy character would be like that. We also got to swoon over the stars of some of our favorite shows as we spied them throughout the room. There was David Carradine who was barefoot at one end; I felt like some Chinese mystical music should have been playing at that moment. I loved the Shaolin monk character he played. Peter Falk was at the other end, and we thought he looked nice all cleaned up compared to his detective character portrayal. We saw Susan Saint James talk to Bea Arthur and watched as Alan Alda smiled all night. It just didn't seem real that we were in the same room as all these famous people.

For the dinner, Chicken Kiev and asparagus with hollandaise sauce was served. There were fresh baked breads, artistically arranged salads, and French desserts. I had never seen such lovely food, or so many pieces of silverware. I wasn't sure what fork to use for each course, but I tried to look confident. We devoured the delicious meal while being mesmerized by the formal award presentations that went on for hours. Wow, what a difference between now and when I was a kid and only ate oatmeal for dinner. Sometimes, I would stop and just soak it all in. Other times the three of us would just look at each other and giggle. I thought it was a miracle that I was among the stars and eating elegant food. I knew that this was the kind of life that I wanted all the time.

Before we knew it, the event was over. We retreated as one of the last guests; the crowds outside were gone, and the night was cold. We were like three Cinderellas at midnight. We bumped back to Agoura in the old truck. We decided it was an unforgettable evening, even if we hadn't been discovered as the next great stars by talent scouts or producers. We all agreed that it had been so cool to do something hardly anyone else ever had a chance to do. The chill of the night made my bones ache, plus knowing that the whole event was over. It seemed like eternity, waiting for the date, and in flash, we were out of there. I hated to go back to my dull existence and life far removed from Hollywood glamour. I knew I had to take charge and do something to get a different life. I knew I would have to take risks that were not normal for girls at that time. What I didn't know was how to take charge of my own destiny, fueled by my dreams and aspirations. How could I propel myself into a whole different reality than I had ever experienced before?

SCHLOCK

CHAPTER 11

There was a buzz in drama class. Everyone was talking, and it was hard to hear what was going on above the din.

"Sheri, what's happening?" I asked the girl next to me.

"Someone is making a film here at the high school this weekend, and they want students from the drama department to be in it as extras. There are even some speaking parts. How cool is that?"

"Oh wow, I'll be there for sure," I promised. This might be my lucky break. I could see it all happening in my head. When films are being made, talent scouts must come watch, I hypothesized. I would be noticed by a scout, who would be looking for fresh new faces. The scout would sign me up with an agent, and the agent would ask me to go to other auditions. Soon I would be chosen for major roles in blockbuster films and become a famous actor. I would have my dream car, my dream house, and more men after me than I would know what to do with. The possibilities of what could happen were exhilarating.

The week dragged. I couldn't stand it. I wanted to become a movie star.

Finally, Saturday arrived. The filmmaker, a local guy who was only about twenty years old, was named John Landis. His buddy, Rick Baker, was a master at making monster costumes. They would be producing and directing a silly monster spoof about a killer ape-man, a "missing link" in the human evolutionary chain from the past who finds himself in modern times. The film title was *Schlock*. John would dress in the ape-man costume, act, and direct at the same time.

Most of the roles had already been cast. I didn't get to do anything but be an extra. The scene I would get to participate in was at a school dance. About twenty of us met at the gym, where we were given directions, and the filming began. Many of us were jealous when George from our class actually got a few speaking lines. His name would go on the credits.

"Action!" came the call. My friend Sheri and I laughed and danced as the music blasted. No one was really dancing as couples; we all just rocked out to Led Zeppelin's "Immigrant Song" while having a great time.

The monster, Schlock, crashed in. Shocked, we screamed and ran about.

"Cut! Do it again, and run back and forth to the doors, like you're trying to get out!" Landis yelled.

We did it a second time. This time it all went well. We watched as some individual encounters with Schlock were filmed, like when Schlock smashed a box of donuts in our classmate Jim's face.

Soon the scenes they needed for the day were completed. Other scenes would be filmed the next day. It all happened quickly and efficiently, and then the excitement was over. No one talked about it much because we knew it would take time for the movie to be finalized. Other scenes had to be filmed at other locations, the film editing would be next, and then they would need to market the finished product.

Many months later, I heard that *Schlock* was being shown at theatres. My friends saw it and told me about it, and I danced around in a little circle. They said I could clearly be seen in the dance scene. I beamed, knowing that I was on the "big screen." I ached with eagerness to see it. Agoura had plenty of upper-middle-class families, so my friends were always running off to the movies or spending money shopping. Our family was still barely scraping by. Money was always short and going to the theatre was an extravagance I didn't get to do. I worked to earn the money. By the time I had saved up enough from ironing and babysitting to buy a ticket on my own, the film was not showing anymore. It was only in the theatres for a week or two. I never got to see the movie on the big screen. Tears would well up in my eyes and I would mope around when my friends talked about it. It was just a reminder of one more way that I felt different from everyone else.

Of course, I didn't get my lucky break by acting in this film. *Schlock* didn't change my life as I had dreamed. I had completely forgotten I was in the film until years later, when I was a professor of anthropology. One of my old classmates on Facebook made a reference to the film, and it made me remember. Not surprisingly, John Landis went on to become a huge success with other films he directed, such as *National Lampoon's Animal House*, *The Blues Brothers*, *An American Werewolf in London*, *Trading Places*, *Three Amigos*, *Coming to America*, and *Beverly Hills Cop III*, and also for directing Michael Jackson's music videos for "Thriller" and "Black or White." Rick Baker won Academy Awards seven times for his master costume and make-up skills.

I found a DVD copy of the film for sale on the internet and bought it. It was only available as a collector film because the filmmakers had become so famous. Finally, I got to see it. Yep, I was there dancing away in my svelte teenage beauty. I was surprised that the dance scene music was different, with some saxophone-y, fifties-like song playing in the background instead of the Led Zeppelin that I remembered. I laughed remembering how I thought this movie would change my life. Then a crazy thought occurred to me. It just *might* have changed my life. I had no idea that anthropology existed as a discipline when I participated in this film, and at the time, I certainly had no intention of becoming a college professor. I didn't know anything about the idea of a "missing link," or that looking for the "missing link" by discovering fossils that document how we became humans through evolutionary time was a part of anthropology. Did the film somehow subliminally influence my choice of studying human evolution? I'd like to believe that. I'd like to think that a tiny seed, a curiosity about human ancestry, was planted in my brain. As a small gesture of gratitude, I make of point of showing the film to a new generation of students on a slow day in our laboratory class each semester. It is always so well received. Perhaps John Landis would be pleased to know that *Schlock* is now a sought-after "cult" film with my students. I hear it is available on Blu-ray now.

JOHN LANDIS
SCHLOCK
"A MONSTER COMEDY ABOUT
AN APE-MAN WHO GOES BANANAS
UNTIL HE FALLS IN LOVE WITH
A BEAUTIFUL BLIND GIRL WHO
THINKS HE'S A DOG..."
WORLD Magazine
DVD

Schlock DVD

LOVE IS A TWO-WAY STREET

CHAPTER 12

I was boy crazy from junior high school times, maybe even before. I fell in love with Terry in kindergarten at Goleta Union Elementary. He was the first crush I ever had. I remember his silky, straight blond hair, and that I kissed him with a quick peck on the lips on the playground. I got a quick rush and knew it was such a bold move for a young child. At that time, girls never made a first move in relationships, but I didn't know my gender rules yet. I didn't even know what relationships were. I just wanted to kiss him. We would often play on the swings and then he would chase me around the big grassy schoolyard. Being at school and laughing with Terry was where I was happy, not at home with the fighting and stress. It was great to have attention, and I was sure I was going to marry this boy who made me want to dance around. I always had so much energy around him. Then, the bad news came. My parents were getting a divorce, and we had to move. I didn't even get to say goodbye because one day we just stopped going to school until after the move. Of course, the divorce was a shocking experience for me, but also it was doubly painful because I missed Terry, and I thought I would never fall in love again. While I missed my dad so much, because he rarely came to visit, there was an ache in my heart for the boy who had given me attention. I guess this taught me at an early age that love is painful, and sometimes a girl doesn't get what she wants, and even if she does, it might not last. The message I got was that the guys I love disappear.

The years of turmoil after my parents' divorce left me a lonely, maladjusted child. I became shy and quiet, and I slipped out of reality to read fairy tales. It gave me hope that someday my Prince Charming, who must be out there, would save me from my situation and that I would have a "happily ever after" life. I knew there was plenty of time since I was just a grade-schooler. We moved from town to town, sometimes more than once in a school year, as my mom adjusted to being a single mom. Mostly she was avoiding bill collectors and critics of her lifestyle. I tried not to develop friendships or romantic interests, since I knew I would be leaving them behind.

When my mom married my stepfather, Bob, things got more stable. After the move to Agoura and staying in the same school district for a few years, I let my guard down. I felt those pangs of longing for love, and in high school, I thought I had finally found the man who would save me.

As a tall, thin, and big, bright-eyed teenager, I was starting to attract guys easily, especially after I became a majorette. I had one boyfriend after another. These were mostly superficial relationships, with some making out happening whenever possible. I loved to kiss, but no one really made me feel the zing I'd felt in kindergarten when I kissed Terry. I wasn't sure if I would ever feel that thrill again. Then, one day at school, I saw him.

He was good looking, had Beatles-length hair, and a broad smile that caught my eye. There was something else, though, and I couldn't put my finger on it. Maybe it was the same blond-colored hair that Terry had? Maybe it was the way he moved around? I just wanted to watch him. I became mesmerized. I would sit in the lunch area, many times alone, to watch. I had to be careful, because I didn't want people to think I was some kind of creepy stalker. He was a student worker in one of the lunch lines, and I would marvel at his energy, as he swiftly moved from place to place, preparing each person's assemblage of milk cartons, chips, lunch-meat sandwiches, hot dogs, and Twinkies. I watched him smile and laugh with the other students in line, and I would giggle. I loved his smile. What was his name, I wondered? I would get red and embarrassed whenever he looked in my direction, believing he knew I was watching him. I asked Jen about him one day.

"Hi Jen." I looked at her tray of food at lunch and said, "Do you really like those rubbery sandwiches? Yuck. School food is the pits. At least you get to talk to that nice guy who works there. Do you see him?" I pointed. "I wonder who he is?"

"Oh yeah, I know him. He's pretty nice. That's Geoff. He's Mark Gunn's brother," said Jen. "I know him from the cross-country team, and he's in the band, too. I think he plays the trumpet."

What a coincidence that I knew his brother Mark. I had been fond of Mark ever since we'd moved to Agoura. He was in the same class as me. He was charming, easy to talk to and laughed at my jokes. We became friends in art class, where we had plenty of time to talk. Although he was a cutie, I knew that Mark was never going to be my boyfriend. Mark was short, and I was already five-foot-ten inches tall. I had pledged that I would never have a boyfriend shorter than me. Even though he was fun to hang out with, Mark was also silly and kid-like, not boyfriend material. His older brother was a different type entirely. He was three years older, meaning he was a senior, taller, and more mature in his behavior. I obsessed about getting to know him. I couldn't go buy something because I never had any money. Besides, what would I say to him?

I brought a peanut-butter-and-jelly sandwich from home every day for my lunch, anyway. I would just watch and think.

Because I was enrolled in theatre, I became involved in the after-school plays. At first, I only volunteered to be part of the different technical work crews, helping with lighting, stagecraft, and costuming. In the first production of the school year, Shakespeare's *The Taming of the Shrew,* as part of the costume crew, Mr. G entrusted me to create elaborate Elizabethan gowns for the show because of the advanced sewing knowledge and skill I had picked up from my older sisters. I was proud that I could sew without patterns. I would pick up the fabrics and trimmings, bring them home, and return with beautiful dresses. As I went in to pick up new materials one afternoon, I saw Geoff in the theatre. What a coincidence! Adrenaline rushed through my veins. I could feel my face heating up and I knew it was turning red. I took a deep breath and moved closer so I could hear him talking to Mr. G.

"We want to have a glorious fanfare at this point, at the opening of the show and again after intermission to bring the audience back to their seats," said Mr. G. As always, he was full of life, using grand hand gestures while at the same time showing the script to Geoff.

Geoff held a trumpet in his hand, and I was excited to think he was going to be involved in the show. I moved closer, ready to ask Mr. G if the materials were ready.

Geoff looked right at me with a smile that made me melt like an ice cube in the tropics: "Hi, there. Are you in the play? My name is Geoff."

He had spoken directly to me! My face flushed more, and I could hardly squeak out my name. "Oh, I'm Fran… ces… ca. I'm… I'm not in the play. I'm just sewing costumes." He looked directly in my eyes. His were sky blue. His voice was deep, and oh my God, that gorgeous smile. I could have run around the theatre building ten times with the emotional surge bolting through my body. I wanted those few moments to last forever. Why did I sound so dumb? I couldn't even say my name. I just smiled and walked away in a panic, not knowing what to do.

In the days that followed, I made myself play it cool. I was determined to be more assertive and not let my shyness stop me. I said hello to him in the lunch line every day, and our friendship progressed. We would talk a little more each time, and I felt like he really liked me. I figured he would ask me to a dance or out on a date any day now, but he didn't ask me out for a date or even to just hang out with him. I thought maybe I needed to be more direct with him. I knew what it was like to be shy and thought maybe deep inside that was his problem too.

We only interacted at school. I knew from Mark that their family lived at Malibou Lake, a tiny community tucked away in the Santa Monica Mountains. That was several miles from where I lived. It was going to be hard. However, I decided the trick to making him see me as girlfriend material was to hang out with him away from school.

"Geoff, I heard you sail. Mark told me you race every Sunday at Malibou Lake."

"Yeah, that's right. We start next week and go all summer long. Do you like to sail?" he asked.

Bingo! I thought. This was the way to his heart.

"Oh, I've never sailed before, but I love the water and I'm a great swimmer. My stepfather has a boat and takes us water skiing. I'm not into the fast boat thing, but sailing sounds neat. I always wanted to try it."

"Come out to the first race on Sunday, and I'll take you out on the boat after the race. It starts at noon. You never know how long it will last because it depends on the wind. You don't mind waiting, do you?"

I would wait for eternity for you, I thought, looking cool on the outside, but running marathons in my mind. "Sure, I'll be there," I said calmly. "Where do I go?"

He flashed that smile that made my stomach tighten up and almost make me queasy and gave me directions to the lake. Then he told me stories of previous racing seasons, which I didn't hear because I was focused on his smile.

I thought the day would never come. Finally, on race day, I jumped on my bike and rode through the old winding roads of Agoura. The ancient oaks had never looked so beautiful, with their dark olive leaves contrasting against the milk-coffee-colored hills. The smell of the sagebrush was intoxicating. Rabbits darted across the road in front of me, and gray lizards were sunning themselves on the warming rock outcrops. It all excited my senses and filled me with happiness. The world was beautiful, and I was going to have my first day sailing with the man of my dreams.

I had never seen a sailboat race and I didn't know what to expect. As I approached the lake, I could see many small boats gathered at one end of it. Malibou Lake was small and a muddy brown color, and I could see from one end of it to the other. The private lake community was surrounded by pretty trees, flowers, and cozy cottages, with plenty of "Keep Out" and "No Trespassing" signs. There was a white club house, the size of a hotel, at one side and only a few open grassy places along the road where I could stop my bike to watch. Geoff told me his boat was number four, so I parked my bike and walked over to the water's edge, searching the sails until I saw it. There was the man I adored. I waved both arms with all my might. He waved back. I heard the announcer's voice, speaking into a microphone from a pier that was on a small island, telling the boats to prepare to start.

Suddenly, there was a bang, and the race began. Like nine white ants on a trail, the boats followed one another and weaved back and forth across the lake to the other end. The wind was gentle and so they moved slowly across the dark water. Back and forth, back and forth, it seemed like hours passed. Then, like angelic doves, with their white mainsails and jibs billowed out, they glided directly back to the other direction from where they had started. I was thrilled when I saw that Geoff was in the lead. As he crossed the finish line, I cheered and jumped up and down to see him win the first race of the season.

Then his boat headed toward me. I got nervous and I didn't know what to do. How would I get in? I started pacing back and forth and ran my hands through my hair. I waved as he got close.

"Go over by the island, there," he yelled, pointing. "You can park your bike by the bridge. Go to the docks and I'll pick you up there."

I jumped on the bike and peddled as fast as I could. I parked, quickly chained my bike, and ran to the dock. The announcer was gathering his gear and a few other people chatted and laughed. Everything was blurred to me because I was focused on boat number four approaching the dock. Geoff pulled up to the side, looped his rope to a post, pulled it close, and tied it snug. He jumped out and came toward me.

"So, what did you think?" he asked.

"Oh my God, that was so cool," I gushed. "Congratulations on your win."

"Thanks. Ready to sail?"

"Sure." I couldn't loosen that huge smile on my face.

We stepped into the boat, and he told me where to sit. He untied the ropes and pushed off from the dock. The air was cooler on the water. It blew my hair all around. I felt like a caged bird set free. I glanced at Geoff and saw his hair blowing behind him. Those blue eyes were so light against his tanned face, and they were fixed into mine for just a moment. He smiled. I was sure I was in heaven.

After that day, I came weekly to the boat races, and we would sail for hours together afterwards. Sometimes we walked around the lake and talked. We spoke about our families, school, and nature. We had so much in common. He came from a big family. He had seven siblings. He had been in Boy Scouts his whole life and loved the outdoors as much as I did. He loved to show me new things, like his garden. We would water the fruit trees together and harvest the veggies. We would play with his cat, Ichabod, in the shade of the trees. One day we went fishing and caught a bunch of small blue gills, put them in a bucket, and brought them to his house. Ichabod came running when he saw us. "Watch this." Geoff pointed to Ichabod.

The cat ran straight up to the bucket Geoff had placed on the lawn. Ichabod reached in, grabbed a fish, and munched away. I gasped.

"He likes his food fresh." Geoff laughed.

"That's amazing! I have never seen a cat willingly put its paws into water like that." I laughed each time the cat would grab another treat.

Underneath all this happiness and friendship, I sensed

something was not right. There were so many opportunities when Geoff could have slipped his arm around me, or he could have stolen a kiss, but it never happened. I never dared to try because I believed in fairy tales and that men are supposed to initiate, so I expected him to make the move. We were only friends, and it would stay that way for years.

Just before my senior year, my family moved away. Since I wanted to finish at the same high school where I had started, I was invited to move in with Jen. I saw this as an opportunity to have more freedom, and to have more time to hang out with Geoff. Jen had been living alone with her father. Her family had suffered some tragic changes in a short time. Her younger brother was diagnosed with a malignant brain tumor and died. Her parents divorced. Jen's older sister, Kathy, moved away for college. Their house was big and empty, and we thought Jen would be happier with my company. It turned out to be a good situation for both of us. We got along great, and Jen's father was rarely home. We were free to come and go as we wanted.

By this time, Geoff was going to a local college and working part-time. With his pay, he bought the coolest car ever, a 1965 Mustang. Now, he came to visit me at Jen's home, and we cooked elaborate lasagna dinners or barbecued steaks together. He made Jen and I laugh and would even help us with some chores like mowing the lawn. Still, with all this freedom, there were no romantic advances.

One night, Geoff asked me to go to the drive-in movies. For the first time, this seemed like a real date. We were going to a drive-in movie, a place where romance blooms. I wore a breezy peasant top with my jeans. My hair was freshly shampooed and shiny. Geoff arrived, and I know he liked what he saw. The tension was killing me. We arrived at the drive-in, and we laughed and joked until the opening credits began. The mood shifted with his focus on the film. I couldn't focus. I wanted him to slip his hand into mine. I wanted a sign that this was a real date. About halfway through the film, he decided to get some popcorn. I waited in the car, worrying about my hair, if I had body odor, if I had bad breath. When he returned from his quest, he offered some popcorn to me. As I reached for the bucket, my hand touched his. It was like an electric current had zapped me. He quickly looked at the movie and focused again. He didn't talk to me, or even look at me, for the rest of the film. When it was over, he drove me home. What was wrong with me? Why didn't he like me? I was at home, more disappointed than ever.

We were at the lake in the late spring; Geoff was showing me how to get in and out of the canoe. We sometimes used it to paddle around the lake, but being a Boy Scout, he wanted me to know all the proper safety rules. He asked me to step into the boat in a way that was unfamiliar. Maybe because I had spoken to my alcoholic mom earlier that day, maybe because Jen's dad was passed out drunk that morning, or maybe because of something unconscious, my anxiety was already high, and I panicked. I couldn't step in the boat. I was frozen. My body just wouldn't respond.

"Get in the boat!" His voice was louder the second time, and I could tell he was getting frustrated.

All I could think about was how he must think I was a basket case.

"I… I… I can't. I don't know why." I started to cry. I hated myself for that.

"You're kidding me, right? Don't be so weird. What's wrong

with you?" He shook his head, turned, and walked away.

My heart sank. I stopped breathing for a second. He had called me weird. I was so stunned for a moment that I just stood there. Then I felt completely weak. "I'm just going to go home now," I yelled to him, and I ran away in the opposite direction. I just had to get away as fast as I could before he saw me crying.

I couldn't get the scene out of my head. I was sure that Geoff would hate me now. Maybe he had always sensed there was something wrong with me. At least, in my thinking, it would explain why he didn't want to be my boyfriend. I was "weird."

I tried to dismiss him from my thoughts and kept myself busy cleaning house, doing homework, and working in the garden. I didn't call him, and he didn't call me. I saw him at some local events, and said hello, mentioned how busy I was and got away quickly before he asked questions. I was still embarrassed and didn't want to hang out with him.

Fortunately, while in my last year of high school, many other guys made it known they were interested in me. I started dating a few, thinking I had forever ruined it with Geoff. Secretly, I even wondered if maybe Geoff was gay. At least I wouldn't be the problem in that case. I never figured it out, and thoughts of Geoff lessened as others gave me attention.

My new boyfriends were a string of rock-and-roll musicians. I was thrilled that the first one played in a garage band. I had met him in the choir at school. We were both tall, and I saw him eyeing me. Ron was good looking, his hair went halfway down his back, like a real rock star. Quickly, after a few visits with him after school, he jumped at being physical, kissing and pawing me at every opportunity. I got a rush of adrenaline from that like I had never felt before. Being touched felt so nice. It was that romantic feeling of pleasure I had been dreaming of for years. Ron always wanted to be around me. When he was around me, he was always touching me and telling me how beautiful I was. I loved feeling attractive and wanted.

Ron played bass guitar, and I would often watch his band practice. Sometimes they got gigs and I would tag along, like a groupie. Once, I even got to go to an officer's club at a local Navy base, when Ron's group played there. I watched the act from the floor as the sailors bought me drink after drink, of which I had no interest. I truly loved the music, and I practiced playing the guitar more. Ron, however, was clearly self-centered and self-serving, a turn-off to me. He was a wild lover, and my first. I had eagerly participated in heavy make-out sessions with other guys. It was the wild seventies and we all chanted "Make love not war!" on every occasion. Escalating to intercourse was an easy transition. Honestly, I have no particular memories of my first time. We had sex a lot. Ron was aggressive, but not abusive, and that was intoxicating. Ron was tall and strong enough that he made me feel small, frail, and feminine. Sex made me feel desirable. I was a drug to Ron. He couldn't get enough of me. His pleasure seeking was insatiable. When our lovemaking was over every time, though, there was nothing to talk about. I soon realized that I was only an adornment for Ron's arm, and a physical outlet for his sexual energy. Admittedly, my own feelings for Ron were not that strong. Good looks weren't enough; this guy didn't have the same personality and chemistry as Geoff, so I stopped seeing Ron.

The next guy I dated, Dan, drank too much. I was too familiar with that experience and, after I saw that pattern of behavior, I hit the road. Another guy, Bob, was a racist who always made negative comments about people in various ethnic groups. When he belittled my Italian immigrant ancestry as "WOP," I ended that relationship, too. In general, the substance abuse lifestyle of most of these musicians turned me off. If it wasn't alcohol, it was marijuana. I didn't want to be around it. All they wanted to do was have sex and get high. I couldn't drink without thinking I was becoming my mother. I loved sex, but I loved nature, and I wanted to be outside more. I also wanted to be able to talk to someone. I missed Geoff.

By the time graduation came, I was still without a real boyfriend and lonely. The week before the ceremony, I took a chance and asked Geoff to go to with me to grad-night at Disneyland. Many local Southern California high schools went to Disneyland after the graduation ceremony to celebrate. Fortunately, Geoff was available, and he accepted. On graduation night, I walked across the stage during the ceremony, after the announcer called my name to receive my diploma. No one clapped. My mom hadn't come because she thought my dad might show up. My dad hadn't come because he assumed my mom would be there. I never felt so alone. I didn't even see Geoff. I was sure that no one loved me or that I could ever be loved. All the other kids had someone to cheer them on. The heavy ache in my heart made it hard to walk across the stage and get my diploma. As I sat down with my peers, I winked back my tears, so they didn't notice.

Afterwards, I looked for my friends, Jen and others, to get on the bus. At least they were going, and I could hang out with them. I still didn't see Geoff, and I tried not to worry. Maybe he had forgotten, or worse, maybe he had changed his mind. Then, like a shining star shooting through the sky, I saw him as he came running. He had worked late and had barely made it in time.

It was the first time I had ever been to Disneyland, and Geoff was the greatest tour guide ever. He had been there many times before and knew everything about the place. It must have seemed like I was his girlfriend to everyone, but I knew we were "just friends." He never tried to hold my hand. He never sat too close to me. He never looked deeply into my eyes. I still had fun with him, like friends do. I loved watching him sing along with the birds in the Enchanted Tiki Room, and we laughed and screamed together on the Matterhorn. What I really wanted to do was hold him, kiss him, make mad love, and declare my love to him. Unlike the other guys I had known, he wasn't driven by hormones. When the night was over, he dropped me off, said goodbye, and sped off in his mustang. I didn't know what I was doing wrong because I had tried so hard to be his girlfriend. All I could hear in my mind that night was the lyrics to Linda Ronstadt's song "Long Long Time." I cried myself to sleep another night.

After graduation, I had to move back with my mother, who now lived on the other side of Los Angeles in Rowland Heights. It was an hour-and-a-half drive from Agoura, with my poorly functioning, gas guzzling, ten-year-old Buick station wagon my family had gotten me as a graduation gift. The journey became difficult, and I saw less and less of Geoff. He made no effort to see me. He was busy with school and work. I needed to enroll in college, too. Weeks would go by and then months passed. Then, I didn't see Geoff anymore. I don't know, to this day, why Geoff was not attracted to me, or why I didn't become his girlfriend. It seemed like it should have happened. I found out several years later that he had gotten married to a girl named Donna, who I had known from Girl Scouts. They had three kids together, and to this day, are very happy. I eventually got in contact with him for this book and tried to ask questions.

Some small clues have surfaced, like a comment recently from Geoff that his mom never liked me. I guess I was not from the proper background and had a troubled family life. I assume that these things were not good girlfriend material in her book. Maybe his mother's opinion was important to him. Recently, as we chatted online, he told me jokingly, it was because I kissed rats. I had pet rats at the time and did kiss them. Then, he asked me why I never kissed him. He even asked me why I thought we had never become boyfriend and girlfriend. I just answered that I thought he wasn't really interested in me. He didn't respond to that comment. This couldn't really be it though because I remember some things. I know there was physical attraction. I only had to look to see that. My only guess is that he was painfully shy. If only I had taken the initiative and not followed the gender protocol of the times and made a move.

Afterwards, when I stopped seeing Geoff, there were deep pangs of loneliness, but I still believed in dreams. I had to rationalize the rejection. I pretended that a relationship with him would have been doomed. I tried to imagine him being mean and controlling, even though I never saw those behaviors in him. I tried to imagine him boring, even though his views fascinated me. I had to think the worst about him and be optimistic about love in the future. I knew I would find true love one day. I fed this dream with pop songs, fairy tales, and my passion for being wanted. These things would get me there. I just knew it. I had no greater dream than to have a "normal" romance.

Living with Jen in Agoura. L-R: Jen, me, Geoff, and Kathy.

THE RESPONSIBLE ONE

CHAPTER 13

After I graduated, I moved back home. My mom and stepfather, Bob, were living in an apartment with my little sister and two brothers. Suzy, Carol, and Ann were all self-sufficient and living on their own. I still didn't like being around the alcoholism, and to escape, I played my guitar on the second floor of a stairwell. One day, I saw a guy walk by. A few minutes later, he walked by again and looked up. He smiled and said hello and walked on. I saw him several days later and he introduced himself. His name was Doug. Doug was kind, handsome, and a musician, too. He played the bass guitar. I felt comfortable with him. He had a kind voice and wanted to talk with me. I sensed that spark of physical attraction toward me I had come to know with other guys. He made me feel like I was special because he used words like "please" and "thank you" when doing ordinary things. We quickly became interested in each other and started hanging out daily. He worked for the Forest Service as a fire fighter in fire season and went to school the rest of the year at Mt. San Antonio College, called Mt. SAC. His maturity and sense of responsibility impressed me. He reminded me of my dad, with his calm demeanor and gentle way of speaking. He convinced me to sign up for classes at Mt. SAC, too. I liked that he was trying to improve his life. I liked that he was a hiker and loved the outdoors.

"Let's go to the desert. My family has a cabin in Joshua Tree," he suggested one day.

"Okay, I have never been there. What's it like?" I asked.

"I love the desert. There is so much space out there. We can hike, and I'll bring my telescope, and we can check out the stars and planets at night. You'll see stars like you've never seen before!" His enthusiasm was infectious.

Doug took me to lots of places, and I got out of the apartment. Sometimes we went to the mountains for a picnic, and sometimes we just went to his friends' houses to play music. Some of his musician friends were losing themselves in drugs and alcohol. I just assumed if you had creative people around, you'd find the stuff. Doug didn't partake in that lifestyle, though. I liked that he was a musician and had not destroyed himself with substance abuse. Every day I liked more and more about him. I liked that he had a job, a career goal, and a car. He was a stable guy.

I started to believe that Doug could save me. I had no direction, goals, or even a pleasant family life. I hated living with my mom and my stepfather. There was so much dysfunction there. I had grown to despise my mom's heavy drinking and Bob's chain-smoking more than ever. Bob had a working class, Midwestern upbringing. His habitual foul language wore on me. I couldn't stand the misogyny and racism any longer. Now I saw him as a sexist pig telling me it was a waste of time to go to college. All I could think about was how I wanted out of there.

Doug was my way out. He genuinely cared about me. When we went camping, in the comfort of our tiny tent, he would tenderly make love to me, unlike the wild rock musicians I had slept with before him. He would hold me gently and always ask me what I liked and wanted. We took our time with our love making and I was relaxed and satisfied every time. My heart melted with his kind consideration. There was a strong bond developing between us. After a couple years of dating, he asked me to marry him, and he became my first husband.

We had a simple ceremony at his grandmother's house in Los Angeles. We moved to a small, one bedroom apartment in Glendora, and I began to work as a bank teller while I went to school part-time. On the weekends, we practiced his passion, searching for petrified wood in the desert. I felt indifferent about the stuff—it all looked the same to me—but it got us outdoors and hiking. Doug was always lugging petrified wood around, and it was starting to accumulate around our patio, but it was a small price to pay. I thought I was finally living what I thought was a normal life.

We even took classes together at the college, like the geology class we enrolled in when I was pregnant with my first baby. In the course, we had to go on a field trip that involved a hike in the Grand Canyon to map the geologic time periods as seen in the strata. At the time of the field trip, I was completing my second trimester of pregnancy. I was in great shape and wasn't worried at all, although Professor Reddinger was hesitant about letting me go. I convinced him I would be fine, and we had a great time backpacking into the canyon while mapping geologic layers of rock. We camped overnight at the bottom and hiked out the next day. Everything went well on the trip, but on the way up there were weather reports of a late snowstorm looming. It was early May, and we had taken a dirt road through the local Native American reservation to the Bass Trail. Professor Reddinger urged us to hurry on the way out, so we wouldn't get our vehicles stuck in snow or mud if it started storming. Proving that I was in great shape despite the pregnancy, and because Doug was a forest fire fighter, we were some of the first ones to the top of the canyon.

Storm clouds were looming, and the temperature was dropping. Professor Reddinger started pacing around. Ten minutes later, as the next group came in, we heard some news. A middle-aged, rockhound participant reported, "Some of the younger guys down there are saying they can't go on. They are exhausted and want to rest. I think it's just that they're so out of shape. Poor guys."

Professor Reddinger started to sound panicked. "We need to get on to paved road before this storm hits. Can any of you go down and meet them? Maybe take their backpacks to lighten their load?"

No one responded. Doug and I looked at each other and shrugged. I guessed it was up to us. We dumped our packs and went down to help. Two other men decided to join us. We found the resting young guys about a mile down the trail and took their backpacks from them. They were pessimistic about making it to the top, and dehydrated. We gave them some water from our canteens and encouraged them to start again. Without their heavy load, step by step, they made it to the top. The air was now thick with moisture, and I could hear thunder getting closer. Just as we drove off, heavy raindrops, turning to slushy snow hit the windshield. By the time we made it to the main highway, the snow was falling steady.

I didn't think of it at the time, but later I thought about the embarrassment these young men must have felt, getting help from a pregnant woman. We safely returned to school, and I didn't think of that event for twenty years. When applying for my full-time professor position years later, the Dean of Natural Sciences was Professor Reddinger. Not only did he remember me, but he also bragged to the hiring committee how I was a former student, a "Wonder Woman." He then relayed the account he remembered, and maybe it even ultimately tipped the committee's choice in my favor. Perhaps it's a testimony to how one never knows how events of the past will be important in the future. Really, I was just lucky to be healthy and strong. I didn't want to be normal and sit around as was typical of pregnant women at that time.

After moving back home with my parents after high school with all my siblings. Back L-R: Ann (holding Denice, Carol's daughter), Carol, Mike (Carol's husband), Donna, me, Bill (Suzy's husband), Suzy (holding son, Will). Front L-R: Bruce holding cat Schatzi, and Brian holding cat B.C.

MONUMENT VALLEY

CHAPTER 14

I went to many new places for the first time with Doug. Of course, as a child, we never had money to travel, and my mom was too busy trying to earn enough to keep us alive. Vacations were unreal to me. So, traveling with Doug felt like I finally got to experience what a vacation was like. We would often go to the desert. He loved the desert and would reminisce about how his family had brought him on excursions out to Joshua Tree since he was a kid. Sometimes we would just take mini road trips around the Southwest. Almost every weekend we would take off somewhere. In reality, these trips were mostly to feed Doug's obsession with petrified wood. He wanted to find undiscovered spots and bring home pieces. I got to see new things and be outdoors and that always made my adventurous spirit soar. It was liberating to drive out of the city away from human civilization. I got to see geological wonders up close, like extinct volcanoes and exposed synclines in road cuts, and of course, fossil beds with petrified wood. I learned about the different Native American groups in areas we visited. I would buy turquoise earrings and beads from vendors on the roadside whenever I could spare a few dollars. The road trips stimulated my view of how I saw myself in the bigger world I had finally gotten to see.

We were usually bumping along the old highways in our hunter green Datsun mini-pickup truck. It had a tiny engine, and we got about forty miles to the gallon. With the little camper shell we put on the back, all we had to do was pull over on the road, climb in the back and we could camp anywhere. We couldn't afford a motel room anyway, and we really liked the freedom of just going where the spirit moved us to go. The accommodations were simple and not always that comfortable, a few sleeping bags on the cold metal truck bed, but the views made it worth it. There was a stillness and a quiet that would meet me in the first light of dawn when I peeked out of the truck to look and listen. I loved that I didn't see any other evidence of humans except the tiny dirt road we had followed. The little stick shift truck didn't have a lot of power, especially with the camper shell, and often we would be grinding up grades in second gear at slower than big-rig speeds. It didn't really matter though. We were in no hurry and enjoyed looking out at the hours of desert landscape as we cruised by. We loved the Joshua trees, the creosote, and the sagebrush. We would see hawks perched on road signs and jackrabbits hopping to hide. We usually saw lizards, tortoises, and snakes basking on the pavement and enjoyed pulling over to check them out. Often, we would pull over and hike out to rock formations to look for fossils. The herby aroma of the desert was a joy to breathe and such relief from a week of choking down smog-filled L.A. Basin air. I loved the medicinal qualities of the aromas, the woody fragrance of the junipers, and the sharp acid-like contrast of the creosote. The earthy incense of the sage was ubiquitous.

On one occasion, we toured the Four Corners region of the Southwest after visiting the Grand Canyon. The open space and monolithic pastel rock formations that rise as tall as the mesa tops reminded me of magazine cover photos for *Arizona Highways*. With tangerine and salmon sunsets, the scenery looked like a watercolor painting. We had just been exploring southern Utah and decided to descend into Monument Valley on the way home. I had heard so much about the place, about the sacred lands of the ancient Puebloan peoples and the contemporary Navajo. I could feel the spirituality of the place. It was as if the ancestors' ghosts were sitting with us in the car. I touched my turquoise bracelet and knew the stones were from the area. It made me feel connected to the place.

"Doug, do you remember the last time we took this road? There is an overlook with a rest area in it. I remember the picnic tables and the view. You can see Ship Rock in the distance. I remember the small outhouse there built with the local stones, and I remember that we never saw another person while we were there."

Doug looked at me and I could tell a question was coming by the way he furrowed his brow. "What are you talking about? I have never been on this road with you."

"Are you sure? I can clearly see a picture of the rest stop in my mind."

"Yeah. The only other time we were out here, we came from the east into Arizona. Maybe you came here with someone else."

"I had never been out of California with anyone since I was three years old," I commented. "I remember that other way we came in too, though. It went through the Navajo Reservation. That's weird. Maybe I saw a picture somewhere. I just have a clear memory of walking up to the viewing area, though."

"It must have been a dream." Doug laughed.

"Maybe." I could still see the vision of the place in my mind.

The road curved and meandered for miles and miles. My eyes were getting heavy, and I was almost ready to doze off. Then we made one more turn and there was the rest stop. I jolted awake.

"Doug, there it is! Just like I described. Please stop." I pointed across the road.

Doug pulled the truck into the tiny rest stop near the picnic tables. We both looked at each other, feeling a little freaked out. What had just happened? I knew I had never been to that spot, yet here it was, and I felt like I knew the spot as if I had been there many times. Was this *déjà vu*? Had I seen this place in photographs and stored the memory in the back of my mind? I even wondered if I had been here in a previous life. The feeling of familiarity and the powerful presence of spirituality made that last thought seem like a real possibility it me.

We got out of the truck and walked to the viewpoint. It was expansive and breathtaking. We talked about how for eons people must have been in awe by the view we were looking at. There must have been thousands of miles in the view from this spot. The valley below was so flat and far away. The rock formations that jutted up from the flat scenery were like islands in the sea. Those rocks were striped and colorful from the various minerals found in each layer, the rusty reds, the pastel pinks, and the subtle oranges from iron oxide and the lemon yellows from sulfur. Colors were separated by black stripes of coal minerals. It looked like an artist had carefully chosen the combinations to create this painting. We unpacked a few snacks and enjoyed a quick picnic lunch while pointing out all the rock formations in the valley below, discussing their geologic origins. All the time, in the back of my mind, I knew this was not a normal experience; it was metaphysical.

ABANDONED AGAIN

CHAPTER 15

The birds were especially agitated in the morning. I woke a bit irritated and grumpy because I had wanted to sleep in. "Why do you birds do this to me?" I yelled.

Doug was out of town, fighting a brush fire in the Sierras with his crew and I didn't have any reason to get up on my day off. Once I was awake, I was awake. I got out of bed and headed to the coffee pot.

The phone rang. I pressed the receiver to my ear.

"Are you sitting down?" my stepmother, Ann-Louise, asked.

"Yes. What's the matter?" She hadn't even said hello, so my heart started racing.

"I don't know how to tell you this… I… I mean, your father has died."

"What? What do you mean? I was just there the other day at the restaurant. He was fine. What… what happened?" I began sobbing. I could hardly catch my breath.

"Last night, I brought him to the hospital. We weren't sure what was wrong, but he didn't feel well. He died in the emergency room of a heart attack. They say that was caused by an aneurysm in his aorta. It's just unbelievable. He was only forty-seven."

I could hardly understand her through all the tears on both sides of the phone line.

"The doctor doesn't know why that happened. I need to call

others. Please tell your family for me."

"Oh my God, I can't believe this is true. I just saw him the other day!" I tried to stand up, but I felt completely weak. I could hardly hold the phone. I wanted to drop it.

"I know. I don't understand myself. Please, I need to go. I'll call later."

I dropped the phone and sat on the bed crying. I remembered my dad's soft voice, telling me how proud he was of me getting straight A's in my last semester of high school. I remembered flying with him in his small planes and always seeing him with that faint smile. I could tell that he knew I felt the same way he did while being airborne. I loved it. He promised me he would teach me to fly one day. Now that would never happen. My heart sank to the floor and became lead. I didn't know how I would ever pick it up. I wanted my dad's big hug that made me feel so safe. It wasn't fair. I started to fume because, God dammit, he was only forty-seven years old. Dads aren't supposed to die that young. He would never know my kids. Oh my God, I couldn't believe it. He was gone, just like that. The news was completely surreal. I wanted to believe I had just woken up from a bad dream, but the pain was very real. I felt sick to my stomach. Then I felt like my body belonged to someone else as numbness set in. My heart, lying in that foreign body, had been ripped out and yet, I couldn't stop crying.

Then, I remembered something. Only a few days earlier I had had a dream. In it, I was talking to a friend. The dream was in the far away future and I was talking matter-of-factly.

"Hi Jen, how's your family?" I asked.

"Everybody's still hanging in there," she answered. "How's your family?"

"Oh, my mom and siblings are fine, but my dad died a few years ago."

When I woke, I remembered thinking how strange it was that I had dreamed my dad was dead. He was so young, and in good health. I shivered. Was the dream a coincidence or a premonition? I didn't want to think about it.

Now guilt overwhelmed me. I had only been in touch with my father for a few years before his death. After my parents got divorced, I hadn't seen him for eight years. My mom didn't want us to see him. She had kept us away by not telling my dad where we lived. It was her form of punishing him for their bad marriage. I had felt abandoned by him not looking harder for us. I often wondered if he really loved us. Living away from home, when I had moved in with Jen, allowed me to find him and contact him. It wasn't that hard, since I knew he was a pilot and loved to fly out of Goleta. I made a few phone calls and got his number.

My dad seemed genuinely happy to hear from me and invited me to visit. I found out that he had gotten remarried to an art instructor named Ann-Louise. He was teaching flight school and working as a private pilot for the actor Fess Parker. After I went to visit him, I got to meet the man who portrayed Davy Crockett and Daniel Boone in films and television. It was such a thrill for me, and Dad was pleased I felt that way. Everything in my life looked better just by being in contact with him again. When I told my brothers I was seeing him, they wanted to go visit with me. Brian had been less than a year old when my dad left and had no memory of him. I told them I would take them but kept putting it off. Now Brian would never get to know his kind, gentle father because of my procrastination.

I had only gotten married months before with my dad at my

side. Before and after the wedding, Doug and I went to visit him and his wife regularly and I felt grateful I had that time. At least I had those memories and the photos we'd taken. Why did this have to end? Why did he die?

Later I learned from his doctors that my father had a dissecting aneurysm in his aorta due to his inheritance of a rare disorder, Marfan syndrome. He didn't know he had it, and the diagnosis was only confirmed after the autopsy. I was told that my siblings and I should be evaluated to see if we had possibly inherited it as well. I was scared. I certainly had all the physical traits that went along with it.

After researching, I found out that Marfan syndrome is a product of a genetic mutation that causes a miscoding of a gene for the connective tissue fibrillin. Because of this bodily structural weakness, one develops physical traits such as long limbs, scoliosis, and tall stature. Abraham Lincoln might have had this disorder. Some call the condition "arachnodactyly," since people with Marfan syndrome have long spider-like fingers. My father and I both shared all those traits. I also learned that the walls of the arteries could be weak, and that retinal detachment could easily occur.

For insurance reasons, I have never been formally diagnosed with Marfan syndrome. With the same physical traits that my dad had, I'm convinced I have inherited the gene. My doctor watches me and regularly conducts tests, like echocardiograms, to check my aorta. So far, so good. Other than my severe scoliosis that causes low-grade chronic pain for me, nothing too bad has happened. Recently, though, my height has shrunk by two and a half inches, partly due to natural aging and the compression of the vertebrae, but a lot more due to degenerative scoliosis. Because of this, more than one doctor is amazed that I am still walking. I want to stay as physically active as I can. I'm afraid if I stop, I won't start again, and I'll fall apart. I have outlived my father by two decades. It's odd to think he was never as old as I am now. When I look in the mirror and see my crooked frame, I wish it wasn't like this. My odd body always makes me feel like a misfit.

I lost touch with my stepmother, Ann-Louise, when she moved to Oregon after my father's death. I last saw her at my father's funeral. Fess Parker gave a heart-felt eulogy, and my family dispersed afterwards. My dad was cremated. I knew he wanted his ashes spread in the mountains above Santa Barbara. I don't know if Ann-Louise ever fulfilled his wish, but I will believe that she did. Years later, I tried to look her up on the internet. I found her obituary, so now I will never really know. I wish there was a graveyard or a specific place where I know my father's ashes were scattered. I believe that the human spirit is closest to its resting place. There are times when I want to send him a prayer. I want to think that with my prayer he could hear me talking to him, updating him on my life events. I want to go to where his remains are to be near his spirit and send that prayer. This is what I would say:

Daddy, I miss you. I feel cheated that you were taken away from this world so young. I didn't get to know you when I was a fully mature adult and talk to you about important subjects like politics, dreams, children, and failures. You would be proud of me though. Even without help, I got through college. I earned a Ph.D. I'm a college professor, and I raised three healthy, talented children. I can see you in those kids, too. Some have your mouth, your eyes, and your charm. I don't blame you for what happened between you and Mom. You both didn't have options like counseling and substance abuse centers, like we have today. I always think of you. I love you more than I can describe.

There is no special place to go to send that prayer. I feel the lonely aching in my limbs when I miss his hug, and I get that sinking sensation when I remember I'll never see him again. I feel abandoned by him again.

When Dad died, I was only twenty years old. It was the first experience I had dealing with people I loved dying. So many more deaths have followed, including my mother's, grandmother's, and uncle's, and some friends as well. When my dad died, I was young, and I looked at my own mortality for the first time. I had to think about life in a new way because I was afraid. I realized that if I had Marfan syndrome, I could die any time. I thought about what I had to show for my existence, what I would leave behind, if anything, if I died today. I thought how sad that we only think about those things when we are forced to do so by these traumatic experiences. The sad truth is that we never know how long we will get to experience life, though.

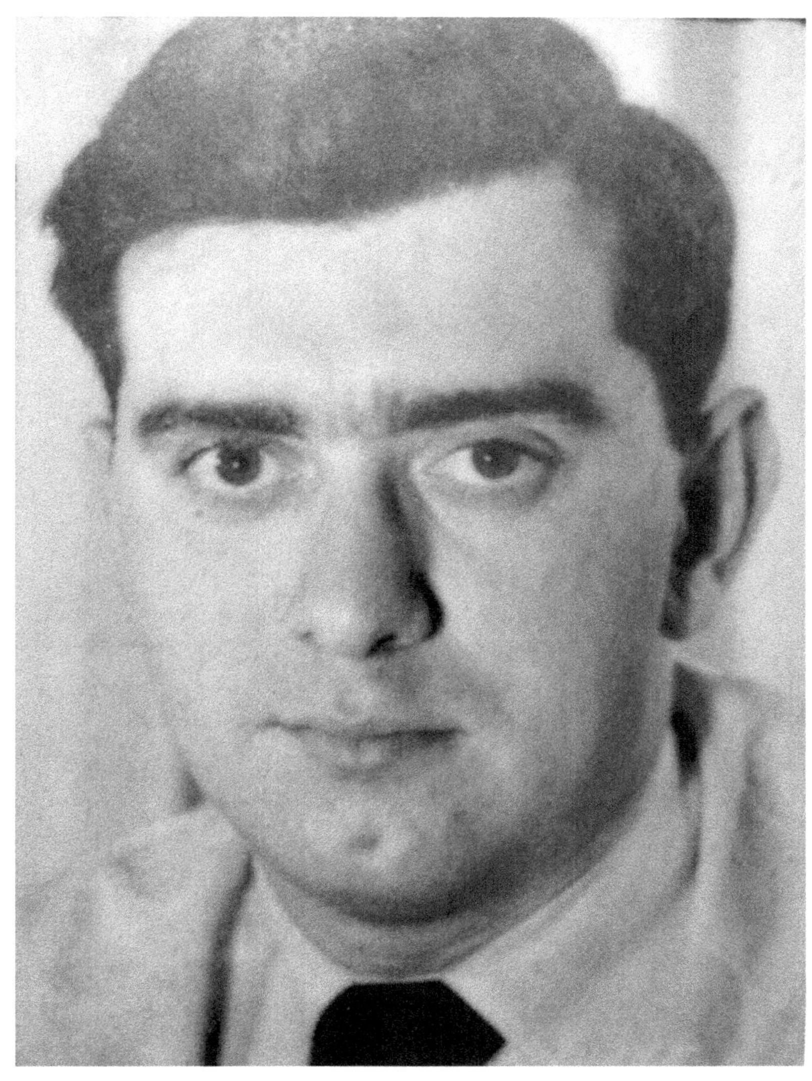

My father

ELUSIVE HAPPINESS

CHAPTER 16

When Rachael was born, I wanted to have a natural birth. I also wanted a home birth, but I was a little nervous. Fortunately, a friend referred me to a birthing center. The rooms were made up like bedrooms, not hospital rooms. It felt like a good compromise. My labor was long, about thirty hours. I was strong and it wasn't especially hard; it was just, I thought, that Rachael didn't want to come out. Finally, I pushed her out into the world. She was a big baby. She weighed nine pounds and four ounces. I was flooded with emotion. I was happy, sad, and in love like never before. I held her close all the time, nursing her whenever she wanted. I never wanted to put her down. I didn't want others to hurt her, ever.

After birthing Rachael, Doug and I moved to a U.S. Forest Service station in the mountains when Doug started working full-time. Tanbark Flats was in the San Dimas Experimental Forest, so the area was closed to the public. Scientists conducted experiments and gathered observational data in that part of the Angeles National Forest. A few Forest Service houses sat near the station and heliport where Doug would be working. I loved the exquisite architecture and craftsmanship of the home that was built by the Civilian Conservation Corps in the 1930s. The houses were made with native stone masonry and wood. Although the outside was painted the typical sea foam, Forest Service green, the interior was all stained tongue and groove paneling: the floors, walls, and ceilings. There were four stone fireplaces, one in each of the two bedrooms, in the living room, and in the dining room. The two-story house was a work of art.

Because of the remote location, we had an old-fashioned party line phone that we shared with neighbors. When the phone rang, the residents of the three houses answered. In one home lived the patrol ranger Bill and his wife Nancy, and in the other one lived a university research student named Judd. We all picked up the phone and listened until we learned for whom the call was intended. We all became good friends. We often lost our electrical power when there was wind and rain, and we had to deal with fire danger regularly. Aside from the few inconveniences, I loved the rustic life, staying at home with my baby, playing the earth mama role, baking bread daily, cooking wholesome meals, and hiking the wilderness. There was always sadness to my hikes, though. I felt completely alone and disconnected from other people and felt like there had to be more to life than what I was doing. I needed some intellectual stimulation, and I wasn't getting any. I knew Doug loved me; I just wasn't sure I really loved him.

My second child, James, was born two-and-half years later. By this time, I was bored with my routine life and read anything I could find. I hungered for scholarly conversations. Doug just liked to do the same things he always did. He would play music with his friends, go to the desert to shoot his gun, or polish his collected petrified wood. To ease the pain of my lack of spiritual connectedness, I decided to continue my education. Because of my two children, I had to take night classes. I had to drive down the mountain, and Doug would watch the kids while I was at school. We never did anything anymore, no hiking together, not even talking about regular things. Most days I did my homework while the kids napped and prepped the evening meal before Doug got home. I felt like there had to be more to life than this. Every day, I became more and more distant from my husband and knew the relationship would end.

I also worked part-time for the Forest Service by collecting information from their weather station that was on top of a hill near the house. The ranger at the station thought I could do this, since I was there all the time. I took readings of all the instruments, recorded them in a book, and called the data in to a radio dispatcher. The work took less than an hour each day. It got me and the kids outside daily.

"This is Francesca at Tanbark Flats. I have today's weather readings for you," I would start. "High temperature is 81, low temperature is 60, wind is south southwest 5, humidity is 12%..."

"Wait a minute, what are you doing out there, in the middle of nowhere, sweetie?" the dispatcher asked me.

"I live here with my husband, Doug Moore. Do you know him?" I asked.

"Yeah, I know who he is."

"What's your name?" I was curious to know who this was that wanted to talk to me.

"My name is Richard, but you can call me 'Dick.'"

"Okay. That was the name of one of my dad's oldest friends."

"Well, aren't you special, my dear. You're living in the wilderness, you know someone else named Dick, and you have the sexiest voice I have ever heard. When do I get to meet you in person?"

He must've heard me blushing through the phone. I liked the attention, but I needed to get finished with the phone call.

"Look," I continued, "I'm flattered that you think that, but I need to finish giving you this weather data. Can we do that now?"

"Okay, no problem, sweetie. I'm just trying to brighten up your lonely day." I really didn't want the call to end. I would be friendlier next time, I vowed.

Each day the phone call I made got a little longer and longer. We talked about Tanbark Flats, my life there, and my marriage. I got a thrill from the attention, and Dick had a way of making me laugh, of complementing me, and filling that emptiness in my soul. Baking bread every day and doing housework wasn't meeting those needs, for sure. I also felt guilty though. I was a married woman, miserable in my marriage, but married. Nothing about this situation was Doug's fault. I was changing. I was convinced I needed to leave Doug and get divorced. I just wasn't sure how that would happen.

One day I saw a man in a Forest Service uniform near the house. He was talking to one of the crewmen from the station. He was tall and robust. I could see he had a sharp jaw line, a mustache, and sandy brown hair. I thought he looked like he could have easily been a cowboy in Western days. I went out to see who it was.

"Well, you're far more beautiful than your voice would ever let on," said the man.

I recognized Dick's voice the moment the first word was spoken. He winked at me, and I felt a surge of adrenaline. He wouldn't stop looking at me, and that made me feel sexy.

"I just came to speak to the ranger, but I had to get a look at you. I see he's waiting for me by the office. We'll talk again soon, gorgeous," he said. Quickly, he went off on his official business. I went back to the kids to daydream about him. Soon I saw him approach in his truck again. I ran out to say goodbye, and he motioned for me to go to him. I snuck out as the kids played with some toys in the living room. As I approached him by his truck, he pulled me to the hidden side and kissed me. His kiss took my breath away. I pulled back and then lunged to kiss him. It was the most passionate kiss I have ever had. I pulled back again and ran off, waving my goodbye. I could hardly wait for our talk the next day when I would call in the weather report.

Our talks became more intimate. I felt empowered and guilty at the same time. I was a married woman, and I knew this was wrong. Every day I discussed my ideas with Dick, and I knew I had to hatch an escape plan with this man who was willing to listen to me and even encourage me.

One day I was particularly sad and called. Doug was so distant from me. I did my chores, and he went to work. After dinner, he would go into the living room and read for hours, and I would go to bed. I didn't want to live this way anymore. "I really need to leave, Dick. But I have no real job, no money, nothing." I sobbed.

"I can take care of you. You're perfect for me. You have nothing to tie you to where you are. You can move in with me," he responded.

"Really? I mean you don't really know me that well. We have talked on the phone for more than a year now, and I've only seen you a couple times in real life, but is that enough?" I was scared, but hopeful.

"I wouldn't have said it, if I didn't mean it," he said.

"I'm not going without my kids. Are you okay with that?" I knew having kids was a deal killer sometimes for my divorced friends who dated.

"Of course. I love kids," he said.

With that, we got to work, and a plan was made. One day, with no warning, I packed my car with the kids and our clothes and only left a note for Doug. It was a horrible thing to do, but I couldn't face the reality of Doug's discovery. It is to this day, my biggest regret. Although I knew that the marriage was doomed and I would never have stayed, I wish I could turn back the clock of time and be more mature and direct about it. Doug didn't deserve that kind of goodbye. He might have been relieved, or he may have been in shock, but I know he was deeply hurt. Worse, the pain from this split and the effects on my kids are unknowable. I took them away from a dad who loved them dearly. At this point in my life, in my late twenties, I was so self-absorbed and concerned only about my happiness. I couldn't see the effects on everyone. Sometimes now, I think that I left because my life with Doug was normal, and I didn't know what to do with that, or I didn't recognize it. Normal had to be uncomfortable for someone who was used to instability. My leaving and the instability were familiar to me.

At first, I was in heaven. Dick welcomed me with open arms, flowers, great sex, and a vocabulary that fed my need for intelligent conversation. We stayed in a small trailer home near Pasadena, in the foothills, for a few months. I filed the paperwork to divorce Doug, who never really protested. When it was final, Dick insisted that we get married the next day. I wish I had been more rational. I look back and see I was like a moth flying straight into a fire. I was so charmed by his charisma. It never occurred to me that I was totally dependent on him for everything.

Things started to change quickly though. He wanted to know everything I did. He wanted to know everywhere I went, and he asked for receipts for everything I bought. I knew those were red flags for an abusive relationship, but I justified the behaviors in my mind. We were dependent on his money, and he only needed to keep track to budget expenses. Of course, he wanted to know what I was doing. He knew I could be flirting behind his back as I had done to Doug.

Dick allowed me to finish school, though. I graduated with my bachelor's degree in anthropology and geography from Cal Poly Pomona and was accepted to graduate school at the University of California, Riverside. Because of this, we were able to get family housing on campus and moved there right away as my classes began. I was relieved to leave the remote trailer home behind and enter back into city life. It would be easier getting my kids in school, and they could have friends.

The housing neighborhood was called "The Crest." The old World War II barracks had been transformed by the university into family student housing, which I could afford on financial aid. We loved the tree-lined streets with no fencing and only large grass lawns separating the houses. It was wonderful to see my kids playing with neighbor kids and not being isolated in the wilderness. All the neighbors were students, too. It was like we were one big family. There was a sense of community, since we all had the same stresses, the same financial concerns and everyone helped everyone. I would babysit for others when I wasn't in class and others would babysit when I had to go. As the kids entered school, juggling school and kids got easier and life started to become routine.

Dick demanded more and more detailed explanations of how I spent my days and money. I also noticed he flirted with all the girls in the complex. He was very particular about everything, and I had to do things the way he wanted. He had to have his tacos assembled in just the right way, with the cheese on top, and the tomatoes diced to a certain size. His clothes had to be ironed perfectly, and the bed made with only one blanket. He was driving me crazy with his needs that I never quite met in his mind. I was trying so hard to do good work at school and needed to focus on my studies, not catering to this man. He was angry at me all the time and yelled about everything.

Mid-semester, I got a call from the elementary school. "Hello, this is Longfellow Elementary calling. Are you Rachael's mother?" a woman asked.

"Yes, I am," I responded, sensing this was not good news.

"You need to come pick up your daughter. She is very sick. She has a high fever. She's in the nurse's office right now."

I drove quickly to get her and found her lethargic and pale, just lying on the school cot. It was such a shock because she had seemed fine a few hours earlier in the day when I had sent her to school. By the time we got back to the house, I knew she had to go to the doctor's right away. I felt panicked about her declining strength. I called my friend to see if she could take care of James, and when she came over, I left quickly.

At the urgent care office, the doctor looked at her immediately and took blood and urine samples.

"She is very sick with a severe kidney infection. We should admit her immediately to the hospital. She is dehydrated, and her fever is very high."

I was terrified. My beautiful girl was so weak and fragile. She was whisked off to the hospital unit with me in tow. She was so dehydrated that they could hardly put the IV needles in her tiny hand, and I cried while I watched. She was stoic and brave. Fluids and antibiotics flowed into her, and we waited. The nurses told me she got there just in time. She could have died from the dehydration. Hours went by, and I finally felt I could leave her side to call home.

At the phone booth, shaking, I dialed my house number.

Dick answered. "Where the hell are you? Sharon told me Rachael was sick. James and I have been waiting for hours for you," he yelled.

I explained how sick Rachael was and how she had almost died from dehydration. "I'm going to be staying with her. I don't want to leave her," I asserted.

"What? You're not coming home to make us dinner?" Dick asked.

At that moment, I felt like I had driven a car into a brick wall. What was wrong with that man? Did he not hear that my first born, my petite child in second grade, had almost died? She needed her mother by her side. All he wanted was dinner. How could he say that? I had a vision of launching carefully crafted tacos at him. Suddenly, Dick was a complete stranger to me. I hated him for all his behaviors, the controlling ways he had, especially with the money and my socializing and his pushiness that was becoming more physical. I hated how he grabbed my arm tightly to get my attention. Instances of his abuse flashed before my eyes. I don't know how I got off the phone, but I stayed by Rachael's side for three days and nights until she was released to go home. I knew I had to get out of this marriage, and while I watched my daughter sleep, and slowly gain some strength, I tried to think of a way.

When I got home, I decided to be bold. I marched up to Dick, and I told him that it wasn't working out for us. He looked like the devil with his gaze of hate on me. He pushed me against the wall. I hit the wall with a thud, and I screamed. How dare he do that, I thought, and I gathered all the energy left in me and stood upright and demanded that he leave. He looked back at me as if I was a piece of trash and he left. I was a different person from that moment on.

I filed for divorce and Dick cleaned out his belongings. I wasn't sure how my friends would take the news. I went to visit my next-door neighbor first. "Susan, I wanted to tell you guys that Dick and I are getting divorced. You probably noticed him moving some stuff out."

"Finally," Susan said with a big grin. I was surprised because I was sure the news would be met with disapproval. Dick had been so friendly with everyone on our street. I wondered why she was smiling.

"What do you mean, finally?" I asked.

"Everyone on the street knows but you, I guess. Dick was a big flirt and had affairs with other women while you were out of the house. We could see them coming and going but tried to mind our own business." Susan looked down at the ground. I sat down and caught my breath. She continued, "I know that he had even fathered a child with a girl over on Peach Street. We were afraid to tell you. If Dick found out we told you, who knows how he would have reacted." Susan sighed. "He really is a jerk. You're better off without him." She looked at me as I wept.

"I better go. I'll talk to you later," I said and ran home. I was sobbing now. I stopped and caught my breath. I felt myself turning red. I felt embarrassed that all this had happened. I didn't like being the one who had a cheating spouse but deep down it made sense. Of course, if he was willing to have an affair with me, a married woman at the time we met, he certainly would do it with others. It was a sickening realization that I was not as special as he had made me feel when we first met. I was now the victim of the pain that I had inflicted on Doug. I swore from that day forward that I would never do that kind of thing to anyone again. I was going to be honest and devoted if there was going to be any other men in my future.

Now, I was alone without a man, having to be an adult by myself for the first time. I wondered if I would ever find a decent man whom I loved. I even wondered if I really ever needed to be in another relationship. I knew I did, since that was what normal people did. I just wanted to know how I could find that mythical happily-ever-after reality. I felt so odd being in my early thirties and already having two divorces under my belt. I just wanted to find that magic formula that would give me a stable, normal life.

I was depressed as I saw myself as a person who would always have relationship failures. I struggled to keep up with the kids' needs and my schoolwork. To add to my maladjustment, my mother suddenly died.

I got the news when I was at the American Anthropological Association conference. It was the first time I had gone to an academic conference. It was the first time I had flown on a commercial airliner; I was all the way across the nation in Washington, D.C., and I was excited about these new experiences. I thought I should check in and let everyone back home know that I had arrived safely. I called my sister, who was staying with my kids, and she told me that Mom had died in her sleep. They didn't know why. I knew her alcoholism was part of it. She drank so much and hardly ate. How could she survive? Again, the surreal feeling I had when I'd heard about my dad's death was back, and it overwhelmed me. It couldn't be true, I thought. But I didn't cry. I calmly listened. There was no pain. Nothing. I hadn't seen my mom in months. I was busy with school, the kids, and the divorce. I thought I would catch up later. I had this overwhelming feeling suddenly that I should come home, but my sister insisted there was nothing I could do there, and I should just finish the conference, which had barely started. I had struggled to save the money to attend, and rationally, she was right. I told her to call me later if there was any more information.

I walked into the next session and sat to watch the presenter. I was still numb, but not for long. Tears suddenly poured down my face and I escaped the session to find refuge in the women's restroom and sobbed. The pain overwhelmed me as I crouched in the corner. I wanted to melt into the wall. The wife of one of my professors, Carol, came in and recognized me. She sat down and asked how she could help me. I squeaked out what had happened, and she put her arm around me to comfort me. Strangers who came in and saw us were worried and then expressed their condolences after Carol explained what was happening. Everyone was so kind, but I only wanted to go home. Carol brought me to her hotel room and helped me call the airline ticketing number to change my flight and soon, with the help of so many, I was back home.

Mourning for my mom was going to be a slow process, I just knew it, since I had so many complicated emotions to deal with. I loved her, but I hated her because she had abandoned us with her alcoholism. She wasn't the kind of mother I wanted, but she was the only mother I had. I felt guilty for not seeing her more often, but I felt angry she never called me. One thing was for sure: I felt alone. I had no father, no mother, no husband. It was all up to me now. I had to get strong. My children depended on me, and I was not going to let them down.

My mom's ashes were buried in the Riverside National Cemetery, near my house. It became my duty to bring flowers there on her birthday and Mother's Day for my other siblings, who all live far away. It's a duty I still do.

HOPE

CHAPTER 17

Some days I felt so light. The burden was lifted. I had a minimal amount of money from my financial aid to get by, but I had housing from the university, and I was in control of my destiny. My kids seemed happier. We watched out for each other a little more carefully. We hung out together in the Crest neighborhood we loved. Our neighbors became our friends, and we all bonded at after-school barbecues, Friday evening family swimming time at the university pool, and walks around the shady streets. I could focus better on my studies without a man I needed to tend to, and I finished my master's degree quickly. Besides being a teaching assistant at the university, I started teaching classes part-time at other local colleges. All these successes made me feel independent, intelligent, and capable. I was in no hurry to get involved with another man at this point. My little family thrived; we continued to learn, and slowly we healed.

On late Friday afternoons for family barbecue and swimming, each family brought their own fixings, which we all cooked on a common grill. There was a sense of community, and setting aside special time with my kids felt like the right thing to do. I met other families there, and this weekly ritual gave us something to look forward to doing. Rachael and James became great swimmers and hearing them laugh with their friends was great therapy to me. I saw couples laughing and playing around, too, and this would send pangs of loneliness through me. I ached to be loved.

I eventually started to date again at the urging of my friends. This time I had a different set of men around me, though. These men were educated entomologists, biologists, and anthropologists. I didn't feel desperate to be in a relationship. and I wasn't looking for any particular kind of man. I was happy teaching my classes and completing my studies, and soon I would be going to Spain to do my research for my Ph.D. dissertation project.

One quarter, while I was a teaching assistant for my major professor in a biological anthropology class and proctoring a final exam for a large lecture class, a handsome re-entry student with a ponytail approached me to turn in his test. He must be in his thirties, I thought. I felt a twinge of attraction but brushed it off to present my professional distance.

"Is there any way I can get my final grade right away? I will be leaving for Africa in a week, and I will be gone for more than a month," he asked me, looking a little too deeply into my eyes.

"Sure," I said. He didn't stop looking into my eyes. My professional veneer melted.

"If you promise to send me a postcard from Africa, I'll send you a postcard the minute I finish grading your exam and calculating the course grade." It seemed like a fair trade. I had a fascination with Africa and thought about how cool it would be to get a postcard from there.

"Where are you going?" I asked him boldly.

"A couple of friends and I are going to Kenya and Tanzania to see the animals," he responded.

"Oh wow. I've always wanted to do that," I said with a wink. "Lucky you. Here, write your address on this." I shoved a piece of paper at him. He wrote his name and address, said thank you, and left. I thought, I'll never see him again, and he probably won't even send me a postcard.

With my normal efficiency, I kept my end of the deal and sent his final grade the next day. I was sure to include my address just in case he came through on his end of the deal. About a month later, I received a postcard with a picture of a famous anthropological site in Olduvai Gorge where hundreds of Acheulean hand axes are strewn about. Early human species made tools out of stone. This kind of tool was made by *Homo erectus*. Usually, anthropologists are lucky to find even one of these artifacts. This famous site had hundreds of them, so they speculate that this was a kind of a stored cache. I appreciated that he had sent me an anthropological postcard. On the other side, all it said was "Thanks, John Green," and nothing more. Well, that was the end of that, I thought, but at least I got a postcard.

Checking the mail one day, about a month after the postcard, I opened a box and found a short letter from John. My heart started to beat a little faster as I opened it up. Again, it was short. It said that he had pictures from his Africa trip that he would love to show me. Would I call him if I was interested? His phone number and name were printed at the bottom. Why not? He was an attractive man, and he had gotten an A in the class, I thought and dialed his number.

John and I met at school to look at his photos. I loved how he appreciated nature like me. He was an entomology major and about to graduate. We talked about our lives and our habits. I told him I went jogging every morning, and he asked if I wanted to jog with him the next day. I agreed and we met up. My jog had never seemed so effortless before. I loved talking to him and his views about everything seemed to match mine perfectly; he was liberal and an environmentalist.

After that day, we met regularly to jog in the morning. A week went by, and he asked me if I would like to go to the movies and see the film *Dances with Wolves.* I really wanted to see it, so I gladly accepted. This was supposed to be a great film because it was a more accurate history of the Plains Native Americans, who were portrayed in the film by real Native Americans. The movie had gotten rave reviews. John picked me up in his classic car, a shiny red, 1960 Buick Special convertible. It was exciting to be going on a real date. John looked especially handsome, not as I usually saw him, sweaty in his jogging pants. I was impressed by the film. It was as good as everyone had claimed. During the film, though, I couldn't help but be distracted by the gorgeous man sitting next to me. I wondered if he would try to hold my hand or put his arm around me. He didn't do either. Ugh. I felt a familiar, uncomfortable let down I remembered from my past. When the film was over, John brought me home. He said good night outside by my door and gave me a hug. He didn't push for anything more physical, although I would have easily gone along with it. I tried to stay optimistic and thought that might be a good thing. So many other guys had tried to get physical immediately. Later that night, I was a little worried that this might turn into another relationship like the one I had with Geoff, but Geoff had never even hugged me, so I was already ahead there. I assured myself this was different. I decided not to worry about it. It didn't matter. I wasn't really in the market for a boyfriend anyway.

I found out that John lived in Fullerton, a town about an hour's drive away, and he would sleep in his camper van at school during the week to save on gas. I also found out he had a girlfriend. It was a rocky relationship, so I think he was keeping his options open. I certainly didn't want to cause any more problems for him with that. I wanted to pull away from his friendship, but I really liked him. A few weeks passed, and one day he asked me if he could take a shower at my house. He was going to be doing an oral presentation in one of his classes and wanted to clean up a bit after the jog. I agreed. We seemed to have developed a respectable level of friendship, and I wasn't worried about anything physical happening between us. I even suggested he sleep on my sofa some nights if he was tired of sleeping in his van. After that, about twice a week, he would do that. I would cook dinner, the kids would hang out with us while we watched a movie, and we would all go to bed. Just like roommates.

The kids were still close to their father and saw him often. They went to spend spring break with him. Our UC Riverside calendar of holidays was different from that of the elementary school. I was still in class, as were the schools where I taught classes. I sent them off and welcomed having a little less responsibility for a few days. John came over as usual, and we had a quiet dinner by ourselves. We threw some couch pillows on the carpet and turned on a movie as we normally did. This time, I could sense a little more tension than usual. I wasn't sure what it was. He then told me that he had broken up with his girlfriend. He looked at me in a different way. Then he turned and gently kissed me. That was it, and I couldn't have wanted this more. His strong arms and big hands made me feel so feminine, and I loved it. We melted together and then drifted off to the bedroom.

Me and John when we first dated.

HELLO DARKNESS, MY OLD FRIEND

CHAPTER 18

A few weeks later, I reminded John of my research plans: "Remember, I'll be leaving for Spain in a couple weeks. I really hate to go now that our relationship is starting to grow."

"I'll write to you all the time. I promise," he said. "I have something for you. I think you could use these." He handed me a small box.

I opened it and found a little zipped pouch and inside a small pair of binoculars.

"Oh, my goodness!" I exclaimed. "This is quite a nice gift." I gave him a big hug and a kiss.

"And here is a bird book for Europe, so you can tell what you're looking at."

I was surprised to get such an expensive gift. I was trying to decide if that meant our relationship had reached a new level. I wasn't used to men giving me gifts like this.

I was very busy during the last two weeks before our family departure. Of course, the kids would be going with me to Spain for six months. I had to make sure my little house had all the bills prepaid. I needed to gather all the schoolwork they would need for the time they would be on this trip, and I had to pack everything we might possibly need. There were traveler's checks to get and last-minute immunizations that needed booster shots.

Eventually, everything came together, and the suitcases were stacked by the front door. I had tickets, money, luggage, and my research materials. This was really going to happen. I had never traveled outside of the United States, so I was a little nervous. I had talked my sister Ann, and her friend Lisa into coming along with us to sightsee a bit of Europe before we settled into our Spanish-Basque village. That thought helped me relax a little.

The day of our departure, I gave John a big hug and a kiss and left with my sister. I felt like he was already committed to me and that he would wait for me to return. He promised to write regularly, and I knew he would. I did not worry about our farewell.

We flew out of Los Angeles International Airport on a long direct flight to Düsseldorf, Germany. Jet lagged, but running on adrenaline, we picked up a rental car and drove to our first hotel. It was unbelievable to me that we were really across the globe in Europe. Everything looked and sounded different: signs all in German, buildings from centuries ago, traffic horns from cars I didn't recognize, and people speaking multiple languages, not just German. The daylight lasted so long, since it was June and at ten in the evening, the sky was just turning to dusk, and everyone we met was eager to help the novice travelers. My experience traveling locally in the United States had left me with memories of people not looking at me and as my mom would say, "minding their own business."

We explored and visited tourist sites as we drove from Germany to Austria, then to Switzerland, Italy, and France. Of course, everywhere we went was beautiful and exotic. There were different styles of architecture, new foods, and new languages for us. I remember moving very quickly from one country to the next and thinking how someday I would like to come back to each location to spend more time there. Eventually, we entered Spain from the south. We drove north through Barcelona and into the Basque region. We arrived at the village of Beinza-Labayen, in the northern part of Spain, early in the day. My sister Ann, her friend Lisa, my two children, and I were already exhausted from our touring the last two weeks prior to arriving. Rachael, James, and I would be staying here for my research project for the next six months, but Ann and Lisa would be going home.

The buildings all looked the same. They were tall, three-story dwellings made of stone blocks and covered in plaster. The white walls contrasted with red tile roofs and stone arched doorways looked like entryways to castles. I would learn that some were still standing after having been constructed a thousand years ago.

Inside the village center, I asked a man crossing the street where the doctor could be found. He directed me to a home, where we introduced ourselves. The doctor was not a Basque man. In Spain, with socialized medicine, new doctors are placed anywhere in the country where there is a need. The doctor had eventually married a Basque woman and was accepted into the daily life there. He then took us directly to the home where we would be staying. After meeting our host family and settling into our new place, Ann and Lisa decided they needed to leave to meet their returning flight home and drove off. I gulped and my heart rate sped up. I was in a foreign country, with the kids, with limited Spanish language skills, and had no car. I felt abandoned and scared. There was no one to count on but myself.

I tried to remember what had made me want to do this crazy thing in the first place. I thought back on how I wasn't sure what to major in while I went to college. I loved every subject. As a re-entry student with kids, I had no direction. I wanted to study biology, forestry, behavioral science, physics, geology, history, and more. I was good at everything, so choosing a major was difficult. Ultimately, after finishing my general education, I transferred from the community college to the local university, Cal Poly Pomona. I chose liberal science as my major, thinking I could narrow it down to something more specific later. I needed to take an anthropology class as a degree requirement, and I loved it. It occurred to me, with the discipline's broad, holistic approach, that this was the major for me. Anthropology was a study of everything about humans, everything I loved, and all of my interests could be explored in this field.

I had inspiring mentors and encouraging professors, like Fred Turnbull, David Lord, and Joan Greenway, who each had their own colorful personalities. They helped me decide to focus on biological anthropology. I really liked population genetics, with its mathematical calculations and focus on evolutionary implications. I have great math skills, and I enjoyed the complexity of the theoretical work. Genetics was a rapidly growing discipline, with the new Human Genome Project that was getting international attention. I felt challenged and intelligent with this specialty focus. As an anthropology-degree holder, I could do graduate work at the University of California in Riverside, and there I would eventually use my research to become a college professor. With this school choice, I could still be near enough for the kids to stay in close contact with their father and work on a Ph.D. at the same time. It was after receiving my Bachelor of Science degree that we moved to Riverside.

Eventually, with the coursework behind me, I proposed a dissertation project which required that I do fieldwork in Spain with the Basque people. My mentor at Cal Poly, Fred Turnbull, had done his project there several years before me, and he had suggested a follow-up study in a nearby village. After dealing with my personal life and divorce from Dick, and completing my oral exam, I would go to Spain.

With the help of the village physician, with whom I corresponded, I was introduced to a local woman, Julietta. She and her three children had some room to spare and could rent us some space. Her husband was a cod fisherman and would be out at sea for the six months we were there. This arrangement seemed ideal.

In Beinza-Labayen, we slowly got used to the routine and rhythm of village life. We found out where to buy the things we needed, where to send our letters and how to access the civil and church records that I needed for my project. Work progressed, and I felt I was a capable scientist. The kids adapted differently. Each day, James would take off hiking in the hills, looking for lizards and frogs. Rachael would busy herself with reading or the schoolwork we'd brought. When the archival work was getting to me, sometimes I would walk the village, drawing out maps and attempting to socialize. I tried to talk with anyone who would talk to me. Julietta sometimes introduced me to people she knew, but mostly she seemed indifferent and unconcerned about us. She just wanted the rent money we gave her.

I was researching the long-time genetic implications of social class endogamy, or marrying only within one's group. The Basque were known to be wary of outsiders. The Romans had even noted it in historical writings. Even more recently, other anthropological researchers documented it. I felt it, too. They liked to keep to themselves. I needed to collect the civil and church records that would allow me to construct family trees for centuries of the village's history. Part of the project also required that I talk to the families to understand the Basque culture from a participation-observation perspective, a hallmark of anthropological research.

Anthropology uses this technique by insisting that the researcher participate in the study community as much as possible to get the inside view of the way things really are. Accessing the records was the easy part. Getting to know the people was the hard part. I had no one to really talk to and the loneliness made me ache.

One day, a child ran up to me and through pantomime suggested I follow him. He brought me to the home of a local woman, Amaya, who turned out to be a young nursing student living with her father and brother. Fortunately, she knew a little English. She would become a great help and dear friend to me.

"My aunt is here, tomorrow," she said. "She lives at New York for many years now. She is visiting home for a few weeks. She can help you, si? Entiende, Señora?" she asked.

"Gracias, entiendo," I responded. I was so happy to know there would be someone with English skills who could help me explain to people what I was doing there. The few attempts I had made in my broken Spanish left some people in the village unsure of my intent. From what I understood from Julietta, some saw me as a government spy. A divorced woman with two children, living in this village in the Pyrenees mountains for an anthropological study was not something that had ever happened in their remote mountain village before. I soon realized that most of the people I had encountered were trying to avoid me, and I experienced those familiar pangs of being an outcast I remembered from childhood.

I was so grateful to meet Amaya and her aunt, Javiera. They were helpful beyond my expectations. They took me to meet the families in the village, one by one, and explained what my project was about and asked their neighbors for their cooperation. It seemed to be the stamp of approval that everyone needed to let me into their world. I appreciated their friendship and trust, and all the help everyone gave me in the end.

Sometimes we just had fun with Amaya and Javiera. We took walks together and gathered blackberries on the mountain roadsides. Once, I even splurged on a rental car, and we spent days visiting tourist areas like the city of Pamplona, castle ruins like castle-palace of Olite, and coastal towns like San Sebastián and Biarritz, France, where we savored fresh seafood-filled paella. We were adapting and the kids were having a great time.

On one occasion, we drove into Pamplona and found a huge traffic jam. The car behind me had been tailgating me and soon bumped into the rear of my car. As we inched ahead, the car bumped into us again. Javiera became angry. At the next pause, she jumped out and went directly to the car behind us to scold him through his open window. She raised her voice, in a way I had never heard from her, at the driver who was an obviously inebriated young man. In very strong language, something you wouldn't expect to come out of an elderly woman, she demanded that he get off the road or she would take him to the police. The young man inched to the side of the road as Javiera had told him to do. I was impressed that he listened to her. It made me laugh. I knew Basque women were seen as equal to men in their culture and a mature person was always respected. I couldn't imagine that same scene happening in the United States, and especially in Southern California.

On another trip over the mountains to France, we crossed a border inspection area with several armed police officers. We were told that the militant Basque separatist group, Euskadi Ta Askatasuna (ETA), had been using this route for arms trafficking. I had never seen so many men in uniform standing with automatic weapons before, and the hair on my neck stood on end.

"Please get out of the car," A soldier demanded in Spanish. We quickly did so, and they began to search our vehicle. Meanwhile,

Javiera walked up to the man in charge.

I could hear her asking him questions, like what was his name, where was he from, and if he still lived in the area. I heard her mention that she was from Beinza-Labayen, but that now she lived in New York City. I heard her ramble on and on about her work, getting old, and all the things she still wanted to do in life. She wouldn't stop talking. The head soldier looked over at us several times as if asking us to come and take her away. We patiently waited for her for over an hour. Finally, the man had had enough.

"Please go on your way," he pleaded, waving toward the road. We looked back as we drove off, and they all looked relieved, shaking their heads.

One day, James came running down from the hills in tears.

"Mom, Mom, they are killing peasants!" he cried out.

My heart skipped a beat and adrenaline rushed through my veins. I had heard that the ETA would sometimes come to small mountain villages and hide out in abandoned houses. I had visions of James witnessing some shepherd that was being punished for discovering their secret hideout.

"Why are they shooting peasants?" he asked with terror in his eyes.

"Tell me what you saw," I quickly asked.

"They had two birds already, and they were shooting more," he said, tears flowing down his face.

"Do you mean pheasants?" I asked. I was trying to get to the bottom of this.

"Yeah, the big birds with the long tails! Why are they shooting them?"

I laughed and laughed. I was so relieved to hear there was

pheasant hunting and not peasant shooting going on in the hills. I wasn't sure where James would have heard or learned the word peasant. I certainly would never have called the Basque villagers by this term.

"I'm sorry I'm laughing because I thought you were saying 'peasant.' A peasant is a person, and I thought someone was killing people, but they are only hunting game birds to make for dinner." James still had a tear in his eye, but he understood.

In August, the village celebrated a yearly fiesta. People from all over the region flooded into town. There were relay races, in which the runners carried heavy weights. There were wood chopping contests. Men would stand on huge logs and chop through them with an axe as fast as they could. There were elaborate feasts, like giant pot-luck gatherings. I saw massive dishes of paella, full of chicken and seafood. There was roasted lamb, homemade sweets like cakes and flans, and so many cheeses. The aroma of all the dishes was intoxicating. Music was everywhere too. Every night, a band would play both traditional songs and contemporary pieces, and everyone would dance until early in the morning. Of course, there was plenty of drinking, singing, and joy-making in general. I was amazed at how this small town with a normal population nearing three hundred people catered to and hosted the thousand or more visitors who wanted to join in. I saw the same men working day and night serving drinks at the corner bar, cleaning up trash, and supplying the make-shift restaurants with supplies. It was obviously a great money-maker event for the town. With my limited Spanish language skill, I asked many people during the week if they were tired. I wanted to interact and get some conversations started. All I got were laughs and looks of disbelief. As I asked a man, Amaya overheard and laughed hard.

"Why are you asking that?" she questioned.

"Because they are working so much. It is so amazing. They must be tired," I said.

"Oh, *Dios mio*! You are asking them if they are married, not tired!" She laughed and laughed. I joined her after turning completely red with embarrassment.

Soon after the fiesta, I was introduced to Alejandro. Maybe Amaya thought I was lonely. He was a kind, single man, and she thought maybe I would like him. I found out that he had once lived in Chino, California, near Riverside, for a few years. He was a little older than me, living with his aging father in their large farmhouse. His sister lived nearby, and we would often get together and visit. Alejandro could speak a little English, which made it easier to talk about subjects other than the weather. He regularly offered to take my children and me to Pamplona when we wanted to go shopping, wander the streets and buy fresh roasted chestnuts, or pick up some souvenirs. Once, he invited me to dinner at his home and tried to prepare my favorite dessert, flan. It was a failure, not having formed into a solid custard, and he was disappointed. Then, from behind the kitchen door, his sister suddenly appeared with a beautiful flan she had prepared. I think they were conspiring to impress me. I could tell Alejandro was attracted to me, but my heart was somewhere else.

John and I wrote to each other regularly. I longed to hear his voice and see him, and I counted the days until I would return and find myself in his arms again. Then a different kind of letter came. After three months, John said that he decided to reconnect with his old girlfriend, and it was over between us. I dropped the letter. My body went limp. I curled up on the bed and wept. I was devastated and five thousand miles away. I couldn't do anything about it. During the day, I tried to act normal around the kids, but nighttime was hard. I would crawl into the cold bed and cry myself to sleep for weeks. As the winter days set in, I felt depression settling over me.

At last, the research project ended. We got to come home to Riverside where we resumed our regular life at the university. Now the work of analyzing all the data was to begin. This slow process of constructing family trees for five hundred years in the village led to my conclusion that landowner class endogamy had occurred. This would ultimately explain the genetic implications, like the physical effects of inbreeding that I had observed. I worked on my dissertation that would present this finding, taught classes at community colleges to earn an income, and the kids went back to their school routines. We were all very busy, and I tried not to think about John, but some things, like the big couch pillows in the living room, reminded me of him.

On a Sunday afternoon, I answered the phone and heard John's voice. It was strange to talk to him after all those months. He said he had had another change of heart. He told me that he had broken up with his girlfriend, permanently. He wanted to know if we could try again. I cautiously agreed. I was lonely, and I still craved to be held by him. Maybe with me here and not overseas, everything would work out. I'm not sure what made me feel this way, but I sensed that our relationship was never going to be an easy one.

John became moodier, and I wondered if he really wanted to be with me. One day, he told me he still wanted to date other women, but see me, too. I stepped back. I needed to look at him from this perspective to see if he was serious. I just couldn't imagine that he was serious. He was. From my perspective, there was no way this was going to happen. I didn't want a casual dating relationship. I wanted a full-time mate. I had no choice. As much as I wanted him, I told him no. I wanted a normal, committed relationship. He said he needed to date around, so we said our goodbyes.

After a few weeks, I forced myself to begin dating other men. My friends brought me to parties and set me up with their friends, but John still had a hold on my feelings. I didn't want to be with other men. No one came close to being as handsome and intelligent as he was. He had so many values that were the same as mine. I thought about how John was from a large, crazy family, just like mine, and I knew that made him understand me better. However, I just had to let go. I couldn't let this man mess up my life. Slowly, I thought of him less and less.

My friends set me up with Steve. We met, got along, and became a couple. He was a Senior Research Associate in entomology at the university, and he was a big hit with the kids. James loved having Steve come over and bring his bug collections with him. He was very kind and gentle. He brought gifts for both Rachael and James and often took us to museums and on other family outings. After a year of dating, he asked me to move in with him. One of the professors he knew was renting their home near the hills, and Steve thought we might like it. I was unsure because I didn't know if Steve was really the right man for me. There wasn't a lot of chemistry between us. I appreciated his personality and his maturity, but our sex life was dull. I convinced myself that it didn't matter. Steve was a good man, stable and intellectual. I accepted, and we moved in together. Love, security, love, security: I was seeing a pattern with the men I dated.

OUR HOUSE IS A VERY FINE HOUSE

CHAPTER 19

The rental house had personality, built in 1960 with a rough, wood-paneling exterior and lime green kitchen counters. It was a single story, four-bedroom, two-bathroom, ranch-style house, and I liked all the space it offered after living in small apartments for years. The house was near the Box Springs Mountains in Riverside. It was on the edge of the granite hills with undeveloped chaparral land behind it. The mature trees in the yard, and the cool relief they offered, made me think that this would be a special place. It was not a typical neighborhood house found in this area, where most are student rental homes, with bare yards: semi-drying lawns and few shrubs. We settled in quickly, loving every inch it offered us. Years later, after buying it and adding acres, it would become my ranch where I still live.

It had been two years since I had last seen John. I recognized his voice immediately when I answered the phone. I was surprised and wondered what could be happening that would make him call me. He asked how I was, and he told me he missed me. We chatted about the latest events in our lives.

"I decided I don't want to date around anymore. I had some good times, but I really want to settle down now," he said. He took a deep breath. "Is there any chance you would take me back? I realize that you are the one I want."

I think my heart stopped for a minute. With so many feelings to instantly sort through, my brain started to hurt. I had loved him so deeply and had grieved his loss with such pain. How could he do this to me?

"I guess it didn't register with you. I told you that I am in a relationship with Steve right now," I said. I ached for John. His words were what I had wanted to hear, but it was too late. How I wanted to hold him. I still loved him. I loved his strength. I missed the way his body felt next to mine when we made love. I missed how we could talk about so many things. I wished I could give him another chance. I wished I didn't have these feelings.

"Can we get together and talk about this in person?" he asked. "I can come right over."

Steve was out of town. His parents had taken him on a family trip to Costa Rica. I felt left out but understood the trip had been planned before Steve and I moved in together. My loneliness and curiosity let me justify letting John come over. I felt it would be okay to just talk, and that's all I really wanted to do. So, I agreed.

An hour later, John was at the door, and my face flushed. I felt like I had had too much coffee to drink, and I wanted to lift off from the ground and fly. I needed to stay calm, though. So, I took a deep breath and opened the door. I didn't want to be disrespectful to Steve, so I asked John if we could talk in the back yard. I knew being in the house was risky. With all that chemistry between us, I might be tempted to do something I would regret later. I never felt this way about Steve. John and I pulled up two lawn chairs and talked under the huge ash tree for hours. He told me how he had been traveling. He told me he had been to counseling, and how the dating of other women didn't work out. He told me that he decided I was the only woman he wanted. What a mess, I thought. I knew that I wanted John. I knew I couldn't be happy living with Steve, knowing John wanted me. When John said goodbye, he wanted to kiss me, but I insisted we just hug. I told him I had to think about things, and I would get back to him. The rest of the day I just sat. I wanted to end my relationship with Steve, but this time, I wasn't going to just walk out.

When Steve returned home, I wasn't eager to see him, and he sensed something was different. I didn't have dinner waiting for him. I hadn't fixed my hair. I was wearing old clothes in which I had been gardening all day. I took him to the privacy of our room and told the truth. I explained that John had been in contact with me, and I was still in love with him. I had not cheated on him, but I wanted to end our relationship. It was difficult to say the words and even more difficult to watch them being heard. I didn't want to hurt anyone. I knew, however, it was the right thing to do. Being the kind, gentle person that he was, Steve just slumped and lowered his head. He did not argue or try to persuade me otherwise. He was not vindictive or hostile. He was crushed, and that made me feel sick. After a few minutes, he told me he would leave. He felt it would be too hard on the kids to move them again. Over the next few days, he packed his belongings and looked for a place to go. Meanwhile, I slept in the extra bedroom. Some friends offered him a room, and in a week, I was a single woman again.

I had to deal with the hard reality of being single. I could barely afford to pay the rent on the house by myself. From time to time, I found different roommates to help with costs. It was stressful having different people in the house, but John and I resumed our old relationship with new enthusiasm. That seemed to make everything good. I didn't want to move to a cheaper place. I loved this house. It seemed to be the right place to be, even magical sometimes. This dream-come-true experience in my life only confirmed that I knew this was not a normal house.

One fall afternoon, I had the sliding glass patio door in my room open to let in the warm air. Resting on my bed, I smelled toast being cooked. No one was home but me. Rachael and James were visiting their dad for the weekend, and my roommate was out. Concerned, I tiptoed into the kitchen. There was no one there, just the smell of toast.

When John came to visit that evening, I told him about my experience.

"Maybe it was the neighbors cooking, and the aroma drifted over here," he said.

"Maybe," I said. "I had the bedroom sliding glass door open."

"Or maybe there is some kind of electrical problem in this house. I'll check it out as soon as I can."

A few days later, I was in the bedroom, and I smelled the toast aroma again. Fortunately, John was visiting, and I called him to the room.

"Do you smell it?" I asked.

"Yep. Let's go walk around the house to see where it's coming from," he said.

We walked into the kitchen and smelled the toast. We walked around the inside of the house, then the outside of the house. It was only in the kitchen.

"I'll crawl up in the attic and look," John told me. He went for a ladder, and I waited. There was nothing to be found.

There were other times it happened. There was no regularity to when the smell of toast would occasionally waft through the house, and nothing bad seemed to come from it. John and I joked that we were just being visited by the "Toast Ghost," who would pop in to make toast and leave. Would the Toast Ghost eventually want more, I often wondered.

It was Sunday and Rachael's birthday. She wanted a lemon meringue pie instead of a cake. She also asked for some new jeans, so I thought I would go early to Kmart to buy some Levis before she got back from her friend's house where she had spent the night.

"James!" I yelled at him sleeping in his room. "I'm going to go get Rachael's present. If you get up, don't eat the eggs. I need them for Rachael's pie."

A grumble came from his room. I peeked in and saw in the dim light a lump under a mass of blankets. Hoping he had heard me, I left to do my errand and returned within an hour.

As I pulled out the needed ingredients to prepare the pie, I noticed that there were only three eggs left in the cartoon. I was positive there were six when I left for the store. I looked around the kitchen and didn't see any evidence that James had cooked eggs, or even that he had gotten out of bed. He was a normal teenager and never emerged on the weekend before noon. If he had gotten something to eat, his favorite pastime in his growing phase, he certainly would have left a mess. Where else could the eggs have gone? My roommate was gone for the weekend.

I opened James' bedroom door, and the lump was in the exact position it had been in when I had left earlier.

"James!" I yelled again. "Why did you eat the eggs after I told you not to do that?" I frowned at him with the stop-playing-games-with-me face.

"What?" James peered at me and mumbled, "I haven't even been out of bed yet."

I titled my head, wondering aloud, "Then where did the eggs go? They were there when I left to the store."

"I have no idea. I was asleep. Leave me alone." He rolled over and buried his head under the blanket.

I closed the door and went back to the kitchen. I searched the shelves in the refrigerator, just to make sure the other eggs weren't there. They were not. Maybe Kim, from next door, came over and borrowed some? She might come in and get them when I was gone, since we had become good friends. Normally, I wouldn't really mind. Now I had to go back to the store to get some eggs to make that pie, so I picked up my purse and went out.

A few hours later, the fresh pie was chilling in the refrigerator. I walked out in the front yard to water the flower boxes. As I pulled the hose out, I saw Kim watering plants in her front yard.

"Hey Kim," I shouted. I put the hose down and walked across the driveway to her yard. "Hey, I was wondering, did you borrow some eggs from me this morning?"

"Oh, hi there, Francesca. No. Why do you ask?" She looked confused.

"Hmm, I wonder who took them? The weirdest thing happened. I had some eggs in the refrigerator, I went to Kmart, and when I got back, some of the eggs were gone. James was asleep the whole time, and Rachael was spending the night with Hilary," I said.

"That's weird," Kim said. "Maybe James is messing with you, or maybe you used them and forgot about it?"

"No, James is like a zombie in the morning. He wasn't awake. I checked before I left. They were all there."

"It wasn't me." Kim dropped the subject and updated me on the latest happenings with her dog and her daughter. I went inside a few minutes later, more curious and confused. For the life of me, I couldn't stop thinking about where those eggs might have gone.

We celebrated Rachael's birthday, and the next morning when I awoke to my alarm, I noticed that it seemed darker than usual for that time of morning. I glanced at the clock and saw that it was four o'clock and not five o'clock, an hour earlier than I usually got up. Someone had changed the time on my alarm clock. Did my cat Milo step on the button? No, because that could only make the time later, not earlier, and to make it earlier, two buttons needed to be pushed at the same time. Maybe James and Rachael were playing a joke on me?

Already awake, I got up, turned on the track lights on the wooden beam in my room and dressed. I sat in my rocking chair and slipped on my socks when there was a pop and a flash and one of the lights went out.

"Damn!" I said, because now I had to climb up on a tall chair to replace it. Pop and flash, and another light went out. Odd, I thought to myself. A lot of weird stuff was happening, the eggs, the alarm, and now two lights popping in a row.

After getting dressed, I got the kids up and ready and sent them off to their schools. I didn't mention the events of the morning. Maybe it was all in my head, and I was just extra tired from working hard. I must be imagining things. There was probably a reasonable explanation for all this stuff. A nice breakfast before work sounded therapeutic. As I opened the egg carton I pulled from the refrigerator, I noticed there were three more in the carton than I remembered from when I had made the pie the day before. I shuddered. What was going on?

I put the eggs back, grabbed my work materials, and left. I didn't want to think about it. When I called John at lunch, he casually suggested that maybe the Toast Ghost had wanted some eggs with his toast, and he had just repaid them. I never found out why these things happened. The toast ghost still visits from time to time. Although nothing bad has happened, I've never sensed that the Toast Ghost is evil. I just wonder if other people have houses where unexplainable events occur. Is this normal?

DREAMTIME

CHAPTER 20

John and I went to Hawaii when I finished my Ph.D. It was John's graduation gift to me. I had always wanted to go there. The Big Island was everything I had hoped it would be, without the commercialism I loathed. We ate fresh pineapple, drank tons of Kona coffee, and camped on the beaches. We hiked the interior forest, looking for endemic birds and marveled at the offering altars we found left by the traditional Natives. As we worked our way inland, we stayed in a small bungalow up in the center of the island between the volcanos Mauna Loa and Mauna Kea. It was there that John got on his knees and proposed to me. With the biggest grin on my face, I said yes. Everything was perfect except John did not have a ring for me.

Everyone who knows me knows that I love the movie *Moonstruck*. Repeating a line from the movie, after saying yes, I asked, "So where's the ring?" John looked embarrassed, grabbed a chocolate bar from his backpack, and fashioned a ring from the foil. He ceremoniously put it on my finger. I knew we were a perfect match.

Soon, after returning home, the planning began. John asked me where else I had always wanted to travel. We could go there for a honeymoon. Without hesitation, I said Madagascar. The place had captivated my imagination since I had first learned about it as a child. John laughed and said he would never have guessed that. He was okay with it, and he would start to arrange it.

This would be my third marriage and John's first. I didn't want a big ceremony, but I didn't want to deny him that experience, either, if that's what he wanted. I was delighted to learn that he had no interest in a formal ceremony at all. We invited John's mother, his best friend Rob, my sister Ann, and my friend Susan to witness our vows where we promised each other we would be devoted until death. The non-denominational minister declared us man and wife in an isolated mountain meadow near Big Bear Lake.

When John and I left for our honeymoon, I was convinced I had found and married the man of my dreams. He was everything I had ever wanted, even if we had had a rocky start. I thought two people could never be closer. As unusual as the honeymoon destination was, we also had company on our trip. Even though I had completed my Ph.D. the previous year, I remained friendly with and frequently visited my dissertation advisor, Al. Sometimes John and I even went camping with Al and his wife Betsy on weekends. They were easy to get along with and enjoyed the natural world as much as we did. Al was a tall, lanky man who worried too much. Betsy was a petite, calm, and confident high-school calculus teacher. They were high school sweethearts who had been married for decades by the time we met them, and they served as a great role model for me and the relationship I thought I had found. I liked how they talked to each other with respect. I wanted to be married for a long time, just like them.

John and I decided to visit them and to share the news about our upcoming trip to Madagascar after the wedding. Al told us how he had always wanted to go there, too. He was fascinated with the plants that were found there and nowhere else in the world. Somehow, strangely, John and I decided that he and Betsy could go along with us, even though it was our honeymoon, so that's what happened. The day after our wedding, my husband and I left to this exotic paradise with my professor and his wife.

Getting to Madagascar was complicated. You can't just jump on a plane and fly to Madagascar. We left Los Angeles and flew to Atlanta. From there we got a flight to Paris. All flights going into Madagascar are on Air France, since Madagascar, although an independent country, still has French community status. From Paris we flew to Réunion Island in the Indian Ocean. We had a few hour's layover and slipped out of the airport to explore a nearby beach. And then, at last, we hopped back on the plane to our final destination. Thirty hours later, from the start of our journey, we arrived at Madagascar's capitol, Antananarivo.

We spent the night in a "modern" hotel, but the room looked like it had been decorated in the height of the colonial period, eighty years earlier, European style. Although everything was clean, the once rich red carpet was worn, and the embossed blue-and-gold, fleur-de-lis patterned wallpaper was faded and torn. The classical Rococo-Gothic furniture was scratched and well used. The hotel had obviously served people in the past with more extravagant taste than we had. Exhausted, we all slept well and woke the next morning to catch our next flight, on a local Madagascar airliner, to the north of the county. After that flight, for the rest of the trip, we would be traveling by truck, camping, and roughing it.

We arrived in the town of Diego Suarez and met our Native guides. These two men, as most Malagasy people, had a mixed ancestry from Indonesia, Africa, and India. The genetics blended well to give them a warm brown skin tone, slightly Asian facial features, and wavy dark hair. I saw other Malagasy people all around me and thought they are an attractive people. Our guides were the ones who would be taking us to our first destination called the Ankarana massif, a limestone formation which had a sinkhole rainforest behind fortress-like cliffs. The wet, tropical climate had worn the stone outcrops into rows of dagger-like points, razor sharp. Its natural defenses, and the difficult and dangerous access into the forest, had preserved this ancient paradise and kept the loggers and the poachers from wiping out the exotic flora and fauna that we had gone to see there.

Our transportation into the wilds was a mini pick-up truck. The guides made it clear, with French, Malagasy, and broken English, that they would sit in the front and the four of us would sit in the bed of the truck with our gear. I started sweating immediately in the sticky humid temperature, and I breathed in wafts of sweetness and spiciness, smells that were unrecognizable. We jumped in the truck bed and headed out, bumping down dirt roads past colorful marketplaces where vendors sold vegetables, straw hats, and fragrant spices. We traveled down winding paths through the broken sweltering rain forest, crossing through villages packed with tiny houses made of bamboo and palm fronds. People who walked along the roads were barefoot, and their clothes were tattered and dirty. I tried to absorb all that was going on and kept thinking about how I had never seen poverty like this before. “I can’t believe how many children I see everywhere!” I pointed out the obvious.

Al said, “I read in the guidebook that Madagascar has one of the highest birthrates in the world and half the population is under age fourteen.” So many mouths to feed! It is no wonder the deforestation of the island was escalating and only a little of the original forest remained. The people seemed unaware of the loss that this would bring. How can you tell a man not to clear some land to plant a crop that will feed his family, though? I wondered how this exotic place might be saved.

I looked again at the strong, willowy people walking the roads with poise and dignity. Some carried a few goods on their heads meant for the marketplace, oblivious to our car as it passed. I thought about my privileged status as a rich foreigner, even though I had never thought of myself that way before. I had so many resources at my disposal and wondered how they managed to eke out a living every day with so little. I looked again and saw a group of teenage girls who were laughing at some joy unknown to me. I saw people who worked and socialized together in the fields, hoeing the vegetable gardens to clear the fast-growing weeds, and sweeping a pathway in a village. I saw that community and thought about how no one in our neighborhood ever talks to anyone. The long journey with nonstop viewing gave me plenty to think about. Maybe our capitalistic society, acquiring nothing but material possessions, was not the road to happiness as I had been taught to believe.

Finally, after six hours on the road, and our aching bodies barely able to take any more, we arrived at Ankarana. Our guides quickly prepared our simple meal of mostly rice with a bit of vegetables and fish, the typical Madagascar meal, although they would rarely have fish. As hungry as we were, it tasted like a gourmet meal. I was grateful for food. I wondered how many we had seen on the journey that didn't have any. Even though I was exhausted, I thought I wouldn't be able to sleep in our tiny tent with so much to think about. I needed to rest and be ready to embark on our first hike into the unknown. I closed my eyes, and in what felt like a blink of time, woke to the bright morning light.

After some coffee and a granola bar, we began our walk. It was still fairly cool, but again, the humidity was great. I had a vague memory of having heard it rain in the night, as it came down every night I learned, and as the day heated up, the forest became steamier. The air was so dense it was difficult to breathe. It felt like I was trying to breathe underwater. We had to be wary and watch out for snakes, poisonous insects, and land leeches, which were everywhere. We were equipped with backpacks full of food, water, flashlights, bug repellents, and some first-aid items. We carried cameras, binoculars, field guides, and walking sticks. All our gear weighed more each minute we continued.

Our enthusiasm was heightened by each encounter with new animals and plants. Some plants were bizarre, looking like they belonged in a make-believe illustration from a Dr. Suess book. Birds were exotic and colorful, singing sweet songs that echoed through the trees. Some animals looked familiar, related to common kinds we had seen in zoos. Some animals were unique, like the lemurs.

Seeing lemurs in the wild was spectacular. All my life I had wanted to see them, and it was unbelievable that I was there, looking at them in their native habitat. We saw the nocturnal sportive lemurs, sleeping in the crooks of branches. They looked like cuddly teddy bears. We saw the common brown lemur leaping through the branches. We even saw the endangered crowned lemurs, with their golden-colored, tiara-looking fur on their heads. Our guides had lured some of them close to us with bananas so that we could get a good look and take photos.

We all laughed, cheered, chatted, and climbed through the limestone and vines, having a wonderful time. Then ahead of me on the trail, I saw John slip and lose his balance.

"Oh crap! I cut my leg!" he yelled.

I didn't think it would be a big deal, because it looked like he had barely fallen from my perspective. As I approached, I could see a tremendous amount of blood pooling on his inner thigh through a tear in his pants. The gash from the razor-sharp stone was deep. John pressed on the wound, and I started to feel a little panic inside. With my knowledge of anatomy, it looked like he could have cut his femoral artery. If that was the case, stopping the bleeding would be difficult, or impossible, and he could die. I felt my heart race. I was thinking how we had hiked into the forest for several hours, and the nearest hospital, if there was one, was another six-hour drive away in Diego Suarez.

The guides, Al, and Betsy all gathered around John. There was a bit of chaos, as everyone realized this could be very serious, trying to think of what to do. The guides started to dig through their back packs. One pulled out a bandana, one a canteen of water. Betsy, who was calm and decisive, had produced a first-aid kit from her pack and was already helping John. Al sprawled out on the ground and worried and fretted. He must have realized, though, that Betsy was in control of the situation and soon things would be fine. All I could imagine, as I paced around sweating even more, not wanting to get in the way of the first-aid attempts, was that I might become a widow after only a few days of marriage.

"I've got some band aids here, and I think we can pull the cut together and keep it closed with them," Betsy declared as she got right to work as if a trained medical practitioner. I knelt next to John, and he grabbed my hand. I could feel him shaking. After a few minutes, the wound was bandaged up, and it looked like the bleeding would stop.

"That's a deep cut. We need to get you somewhere so you can get some stitches," Betsy advised.

"Maybe we should cancel the rest of trip and go back home?" I questioned.

"I'd rather die here in the forest than get back on that cramped plane for a thirty-hour trip," John said.

The guides agreed that John needed to get some medical help, so they directed us back on the trail that would lead to the truck. It was a slower walk back. John was in intense pain, but he managed to make it the entire way with all of us taking turns supporting him. We arrived back to the truck at dusk. We quickly nibbled on some more granola bars, and we were ready to go. John would ride in the cab of the truck this time. There was nothing to see in the dark, and after another six-hour drive, this time with heavy hearts and wild imaginations, we made it back to Diego Suarez.

Since it was the middle of the night, the guides took us to a local doctor's house. They woke him, and he told us to meet him at his clinic. The guides knew where to go, and we depended on them to help in every way, especially since we did not speak the Malagasy language. We were all frightened and exhausted. We felt a little relief knowing that there was a medical doctor who would see John.

The clinic looked like something out of an old movie set from a film about colonial Africa. The make-shift building had some concrete walls, joined with pieces of corrugated tin, old tires, recycled lumber, and cardboard. The patient area appeared somewhat clean, with shelves of old towels, and only a few medical supplies. The metal examination table was in the center of the room. There were muddy foot tracks on the floor, and the tables were full of opened boxes with unorganized instruments. The room smelled like antiseptic and rotting flesh. Off to one side, there were some rags with bloodstains sitting in a white enamel basin. My stomach turned, and I begged myself not to throw up. I tried to convince myself that everything would be fine. I worried about the level of hygiene in this facility, what kind of exotic pathogens were hiding there, and what microscopic things I couldn't see. I worried about what would happen to John and if he would end up with a serious infection and risk his life.

The half-asleep doctor came in and hardly spoke. At least, when he did speak, he spoke in English. Drenching the wound with Betadine, he stitched it closed with no anesthesia. John endured the procedure stoically. My heart ached with empathy and concern for my husband. I tried to remember why I had wanted to go to this remote destination. After covering the wound with bandages and giving him a shot of penicillin, the doctor advised John to get a daily penicillin injection, and to change the bandages regularly. He would not need a prescription to get the antibiotics in Madagascar; he would just have to go to a pharmacy and buy it. The cost was beyond the means of most residents, whose average yearly income is only around two hundred dollars, so there was little danger of overuse or misuse of these drugs here. We would also have to find a trained health worker to give him this injection each day. After the doctor finished, and we paid for his services, we left for an unplanned night at a small hotel.

Our adventure in Madagascar continued, despite John's injury. We saw new and different animals and plants at each place we visited, although we moved at a slower pace. The lemurs are always a delight to see. My favorite being the sifakas, who bounce on the ground in a Russian-like sashay dance move. They live in the thorny forest of the south. The trees there are lined with strings of thorns, and it is thrilling to watch the sifakas jump from one to the other, like watching circus acrobats. We tried to see fossas, but to no avail. They are nocturnal stealthy lemur predators related to the mongoose, and rarely do humans see them.

My favorite plants were the different species of baobab trees. They were huge and awe inspiring in the way that I felt like I was standing next to a giant sequoia tree. I knew that they stored water in their bark for the dry season, and their fruit was a known delicacy. Admiring one, the guide told me a Malagasy story about how God had become angry with the trees for being proud and conceited, and so as punishment he uprooted them and put them back in the ground upside down. They really did look like upside-down trees, especially in the cool dry season when we were there, with their leafless branches. I still photographed them silhouetted in front of a ruby red sunset. We enjoyed ticking off our list of the new animals and plants we saw and marveled at each new find.

John got his daily injections for four weeks as we moved from town to town, and he stayed healthy. He got to ride in the truck cab, to protect his injury and because it was difficult to climb in and out of the back. I missed chatting with him as we drove along, but Al and Betsy were still there with me. I, on the other hand, did not stay well. Without the protection of the daily antibiotics that John was taking, I ended up very sick, so neither of us escaped unscathed.

One day near the end of our trip, as we were bouncing along in the back of the truck, I leaned over to Betsy, and whispered, "I think I'm going to faint." I was dehydrated and lightheaded. I realized I probably had dysentery. The next I was aware, I was lying on the ground, and John was looking down at me. I had fainted. I figured they had stopped the truck, taken me out, and helped me come back to consciousness. After a rehydration drink, I sat up, and I felt a sticky wetness in my jeans. Oh no, I didn't want to think about that. When I had fainted, I had relaxed every muscle in my body.

"John, come closer!" I whispered. He leaned over me.

"What's the matter?" he questioned.

"Um, I… I… I shit my pants!" I felt embarrassed, as the words left my mouth. I was still feeling dizzy. How could I stand up to change and clean myself without fainting again?

"Don't worry. I'll help you take care of that," he said. It was as if he was reading my mind.

John asked Betsy to pull out some clean clothes from my backpack, and he gathered some water bottles and a small towel. He helped me carefully get up from the ground, and we slowly walked off to some nearby bushes. Once hidden from the others, John helped me undress, clean myself, and put on clean clothes. He was as kind and gentle as anyone could be, even though I was mortified that someone had to help clean up my shit. I had never been so intimate with anyone regarding this bodily function. I was so grateful he was doing this though, and I thought if he was willing to help me with this, it was a sign that our marriage would last forever, "through sickness and through health."

Ultimately, the health issues we faced were a small price to pay for the experience of an unforgettable time. Once home, I quickly recovered with a dose of antibiotics. John's wound would take a long time to heal, and many trips were needed to his personal doctor. After about a year, it finally developed into a large scar, which we jokingly call, the "Madaga-scar."

The trip had affected my conscience. When I got home, I needed to go to the grocery store to stock up on the usual food stuff. I got to the cereal row as I picked up regular staples. There, I saw healthy ones, sugary ones, high-fiber varieties, name brands, store brands, and more, all neatly arranged. There were big boxes and small boxes of every kind of cereal imaginable. The row seemed endless, towering with tons of food. I stopped in awe, as if I was seeing cereal for the first time in my life. How many of these boxes would go to waste, I wondered. I felt a pang of disgust in my stomach. Why do we have so much? Why do we waste so much when people in Madagascar have so little food to eat, yet we are so unhappy compared to them? I was experiencing a kind of reverse culture shock in my own country, my own town, my regular supermarket. It was just the beginning for me in evaluating my lifestyle. I was seeing conspicuous consumption and waste as never before. My worldview and subsequent personal behaviors would never be the same. I became a serious, conscious consumer from that point on. John was already an environmentalist, so he agreed with me on these issues and that deepened the bond for the man of my dreams. Unlike most Americans, we decided to reject the capitalistic values of throwing away usable things and relentlessly buying more and more.

Wedding day for me and John

In Madagascar with ring tailed lemurs

UNIVERSITY OF CALIFORNIA, RIVERSIDE
Commencement June 18, 1994

Ph.D. Graduation Day at UCR

DISASTROUS DRIVE

CHAPTER 21

While in Madagascar, we had met a couple from Britain, Joe and Alyson. They were about our age, and both were teachers. Joe taught high-school biology and Alyson taught primary grades. Joe had red hair and a beard with a typical pale British complexion. He was witty, although hard to understand with his thick Midlands accent. Alyson was more of a Jane Goodall type, hair in a ponytail, athletic with a clearer, more London-type English accent. Both loved nature as much as John and I did. We enjoyed their company on a side trip where we saw other lemurs. We knew they were our kind of people when we saw them reading an Edward Abbey book, *The Monkey Wrench Gang*. I also noticed Alyson wore mismatched socks, a clear sign we would all get along well. After our return home, we kept in touch with them and decided to travel with them periodically. The following year, we took them on a tour of the Southwest United States, visiting places mentioned in the book, *The Monkey Wrench Gang*. On that trip we decided to travel to Alaska.

John and I had always wanted to visit this wilderness state, and the Brits were excited to join us on the adventure. When I thought about Alaska, I couldn't help but envision great expanses of open land, wild animals and long, almost unending summer days. Alaska was still wild. There was plenty of wilderness with few people. These qualities made it the perfect travel destination for all of us. I eagerly waited for this new adventure to begin.

I was teaching summer school classes, so John and the Brits would start without me. Since they were driving up the coast of California, from Riverside, through Oregon and Washington, to British Columbia, it would take some time. I had been to many of the coastal stops in the past, but this was all new for our friends. Then, when classes were over, I would fly north with Rebecca, who was just a toddler, and meet them in Ketchikan. They had caught the Inside Passage ferry, and Ketchikan was one of the usual stops. Rebecca and I arrived the night before the others did, so while we waited for them, we visited the Totem Heritage Center. I taught classes on Native Americans and thought this would be a great place to learn something new.

I was captivated and at the same time saddened by my visit with the ancient totem poles. The minute I walked into the gallery I felt a weight on me that was more than the toddler I was holding. Maybe some ancient genes in me had awoken and shook my emotions. There they were, the totem poles, lying on their sides instead of standing tall. I felt a faint energy pulsing from them that reminded me of a dying flashlight. They wanted to be bright and shine, but they were old and spent. They were like warriors from a different time, who had fought to protect the people and their ways, warriors who were now tired. They were rotting and falling apart from weathering, years of neglect, and changing times. I saw them as veteran soldiers in a convalescence hospital. Maybe the museum guide, a Haida woman, noticed my pain. She introduced herself and took the time to explain to me the functional differences and ages of all the poles, even though I didn't ask. I had learned about them in my anthropology studies, but I let her talk to see what other knowledge I could acquire.

"This one is a funeral pole, and is very old," she said. "They used to put the cremated ashes of important people in a box up there, near the top." She pointed.

I nodded and Rebecca, although bored, was content to be held in my arms.

"Because of your respectful appreciation, I want to show you something special," she said.

She led us outside the gallery to an area near a small shed behind the museum. There, under a partial roof, busy at work, was an older man carving a new totem pole.

"This one was commissioned by my friend's aunt, to commemorate the death of her grandfather. It's a memorial pole, with all the crests of the ancestral clans represented by animals and mythical beings from her grandfather's family."

I was relieved to know that new soldiers were rising to replace the old ones, and the culture's beliefs were still guarded in this generation. I thanked her for giving me the privilege of the viewing.

After our short museum visit, Rebecca and I spent a quiet night at a small hotel, and the next morning we met the ferry as planned. We boarded and continued our journey with John and the Brits, who we eagerly met with big hugs. We had a short stop in Juneau, where we all ran to see the glacier before we departed again. It was the first glacier I had seen close up, and the blue ice was like a piece of frozen sky. Back on the ferry, we continued the journey and eventually disembarked with our car in Haines. The first thing I noticed was there were so many bald eagles everywhere. Every way I turned, I saw them soaring above me and sitting on treetops. We had seen several on an earlier stop in Juno, and from the ferry cruising our way north, but the numbers here were unbelievable. They come for the salmon runs, to feast. I thought how they were like house finches at our feeders, in quantity. I bet the Alaskans didn't think all these eagles were a big deal anymore, like I don't think house finches are a big deal. We call birds like that, that we see all the time, "trash birds." I couldn't imagine them calling eagles "trash birds." These are magnificent birds, the holy messengers for Native Americans. When they fly, their wingspan is broad and will carry the prayers of the people to the creator. The soaring birds are strong against the wind. It is no wonder that they also became a beloved symbol for American freedom.

That evening, we went to a salmon bake. The local Tlingit people barbecue salmon on open flames and serve it to tourists with other local treats, like berry cobbler. The flavors were smokey, nutty, and sweet from the local honey. The Tlingit ceremonial site, where the feast was held, seemed eerie and mysterious to me. There was a huge "long house" made of red cedar planks, carved, and painted with the familiar form lines. I thought that the feeling must have come from the musty smell of damp air and soil permeating everything. After dinner we walked through the long house where low beams of sunlight peaked through cracks in the planked walls and admired the carved cedar beams and the painted forms of Raven, Eagle, and Bear, among others. It is, to this day, my favorite art style. The style is rigid, with only certain curved shapes made in red and black.

Driving through parts of British Columbia and the Yukon Territory, and then back into Alaska, we eventually made it to Fairbanks and to the Dalton Highway. Our goal was to travel to the Arctic Ocean, across the expansive state to view the wildlife. This road had been constructed to service the Alaskan oil pipeline. Oil pumped from the north coast was carried by this long pipe to the Pacific Ocean. Although the road would end at the

Arctic Sea, where we wanted to go, it was unpaved and there were very few services along its length. Being tough and seasoned adventure travelers, we eagerly sought the challenge.

We were rewarded with breathtaking views of the landscape. The open space, as far as the eye could see, overwhelmed our senses. We saw all the animals we hoped we would see, including immense moose. I had never realized how tall they were until I saw them standing taller than our van as we inched along. The musk oxen were standing on the tundra, and I thought they looked like they were out of the Pleistocene diorama I had seen at a natural history museum. I was intrigued to learn about the underlying layer of fur they have that is collected to create a fine wool called "qiviut" by the Native people. They knit with this, and it is as soft as Angora wool. Caribou were seen in great herds on the horizon, and I knew that this was an important food source for the inland Athabaskan people. We regularly passed by grizzly bears and did not slow down. We did not want to provoke them. They can be aggressive. We also saw plenty of familiar black bears, the kind we have in California. The Arctic foxes pounced on prey, and many species of birds flew by in their breeding plumage splendor. We were even blessed with a glimpse of a lynx as it sped across the road. One night we heard wolves howling as we sat by our campfire. It sent chills up my spine, but I was thrilled because I felt my ancestral DNA connecting with Mother Earth. This was a sound that our ancestors must have heard. I knew this was not normal, as most would be frightened by the sound.

Eventually, we reached the tree line in the Arctic. Joe and John had an idea at the same time. "Stop the car, John," said Joe.

"Are you thinking what I'm thinking?" answered John.

"What are you two up to?" Alyson looked at them suspiciously like a schoolteacher looks at a prankster.

"This is the last tree we will probably see as we head up north." Joe pointed to the scraggly conifer. "It's our duty to mark it."

"Absolutely," said John who had already stopped the car and was opening the door. Both men ran out, unzipped their pants, and peed on the tree. Alyson and I just shook our heads.

We wound our way onto the tundra after many miles. When we regularly stepped out of our trusty van, our haven, to stretch, the mosquitoes were always quick to respond. They are incredibly large, and we joked about how they were the state bird for Alaska. We scooped up berries from the tundra bushes, so many kinds and so flavorful. My whole view of the tundra was changed by all we saw. I had always thought it was a lifeless, barren plain. Here it teemed with magnificent life.

Over many days of travel, we eventually made it near Prudhoe Bay, to the town of Deadhorse. We pulled up to an area outside of town to camp. We set up our tents, and I looked at my watch. It was 11:00 pm, and sunset. We hadn't even had our dinner yet. The long summer days in the Arctic can throw off your internal clock. No one could believe the time.

In the morning, we drove to a bus stop. A tourist cannot drive around the town. It was built to accommodate the oil companies and the Alaskan Pipeline crews. There are safety and national security concerns that prohibit outsiders from wandering. The bus would only stop at certain places. We observed as much as we could as we drove in. There were gray metal buildings, black tar spots on the ground, gas fumes everywhere. John and the Brits wanted to put their feet in the Arctic Sea, as it was their tradition to step into any new body of water we encountered. There was only one place where they would quickly stop the bus and allow them to run out and do that. We then were driven to a general store to get supplies and a few souvenirs. I saw a T-shirt for sale with "Alaskan Men: the odds are good, but the goods are odd!" written across it. The whole town seemed odd. Was this all there was to see? There had to be more. After shopping, riding the bus again, and passing once again through locked gates, we were returned to our van. This town was dirty, ugly, and depressing. How horrible to think of the destruction of the open tundra for "progress" and to imagine what must have been there previously on the site.

Over the next week, we rambled our way back toward Fairbanks. We arrived at a gas station to fill up. Gas fumes were strong as the fuel was being pumped into the van at the remote station where we stopped. There was a coffee shop attached to the station and little else for miles and miles around on the forested outskirts of Fairbanks. I snapped in the buckle of my seat belt and settled in for the next long stretch of driving after the thousand miles of the desolate Dalton Highway. We did it, we had driven all the way to Prudhoe Bay on the coast of the Arctic Sea and now we were almost home. Suddenly, I saw John running to the van and yelling. I was inside with the windows closed so I couldn't understand his words. His waving arms and panicked face told me more than I needed to know. I jumped out and pulled the back sliding door to grab Rebecca out of her car seat. I could smell the burning now.

"Get out of there! Run as far as you can!" John yelled louder.

Yanking the seat belts apart and swooping up my toddler, I ran away from the car like an Olympic sprinter. John grabbed a fire extinguisher thrown at him by a fleeing trucker and sprayed the engine in the rear of the van. In the distance, I could see other truck drivers running to their rigs and driving away as fast as they could. They knew the whole place could blow up in minutes. The gas station attendant yelled something I couldn't understand, and Joe and Alyson emerged from the coffee shop and ran toward me. There was chaos everywhere. At last, John got the flames out, but gas was still pouring onto the ground. Our van was badly damaged, the engine was burned, and the interior melted and blackened. We examined the car shell and tried to determine what had caused the problem. We had to assess things and make decisions in order to get back home. Depressed and exhausted, this was not how we had envisioned the end of our journey.

It turned out that we had broken a fuel line on the rough road, and when John started to fill the tank, the heat of the Volkswagen rear engine ignited the dripping gas. The van was not completely destroyed, but it was inoperable. It would be too difficult to get it back to California to rebuild it. John arranged for a tow truck to take it to the junkyard after we emptied it. With the help of two local women, strong as any men I have ever known, who drove up in an oversized king-cab truck, we loaded up all we could salvage and found a motel in town to sort things out. The next day, we boxed up and shipped back home as much as we could. We rented a car to take us to the airport and flew home, abandoning our trusty, beloved camping van. Although we survived, it did not.

ANCESTRAL CALL

CHAPTER 22

Spirituality has been an important part of my acceptance and coping mechanism for dealing with my life challenges. I was raised in the Catholic Church but felt it didn't fit anymore with my values. I was bothered by the patriarchy in the practice of it. In college, I was introduced to the Native American sweat lodge ceremony while working with Native students on campus. I'm not sure what attracted me to learn about Native Americans: their history, ceremony, and culture. I did a DNA test and learned I have mixed ancestral genes: Italian, Scottish, other mixed European, Northern African, or Arabian, Asian, and yes, even Native American genes. I guess being a "mutt" has its physical advantages. In genetics, we call it "hybrid vigor," but psychologically, it can also send people on identity quests, trying to figure out who they are, how they belong, and what their connections to life are. I had been drawn to something unexplainable since the Alaskan trip. The totem poles and Mother Earth were calling me. I wanted to listen and hear them, but there was still much to learn.

For our summer vacation, Joe and Alyson were visiting from England again. Even after the Alaskan disaster, they were brave enough to go on another adventure with us. This time, we had driven up to South Dakota from California and I looked forward to a visit with my "adopted" Lakota son, Jayson. As the Native American Intertribal Student Alliance faculty advisor, I got to know him well. He was an ex-Marine, who had some family problems. After a traumatic divorce, he was depressed, and I worried about suicide. I introduced him to our club spiritual advisor, and we helped him to recovery. We have been close ever since, and I symbolically adopted him. Because I had traveled with John, Joe, and Alyson, I had to go along with their plans to visit the tourist areas.

"We have to go to Mount Rushmore!" exclaimed Alyson. "It's the 'shrine of democracy.' Everyone in England who comes to America on holiday goes there."

"Oh please," I protested, "Do we have to? The Black Hills are sacred to the Lakota and the carving of the Presidents' faces is considered a sacrilege!"

John felt like we were obliged to go there and added, "We have to take them there, Francesca. We will go to the Crazy Horse Memorial, too," as if that were enough to appease me.

Grudgingly, I agreed. We arrived at the monument in the evening. We parked our van in a multi-storied concrete garage, walked through the elaborately gated entrance, and proceeded down a paved corridor adorned with all the colorful state flags hanging overhead.

"We've found the California flag!" Alyson shouted to me from a few yards ahead.

Oh joy, I thought sarcastically. I was not in the mood to be patriotic.

"It says in this leaflet that there's a film program at dusk in the amphitheater, describing the history of this place. Afterwards, they light up the carvings on the mountain. It sounds very dramatic and we're just in time." Alyson trotted ahead.

Following at some distance behind them, we made our way to

the crowded seating area. I stood at the back as the others sat down and watched the film begin. The documentary started with a brief history of the Lakota people and their beliefs about the Black Hills and how it is the place of origin in their oral tradition. Okay, I thought, this isn't too bad, so far. Then the film went into the history of the invasion of the area from the American westward expansion. The film's perspective touted Manifest Destiny mentality, stating that the land was opened up by God, and it was America's right to take it. After brushing over the era of genocide, greed, and betrayal with phrasing like "soon the Native population numbers diminished," I walked away disgusted. Yeah, diminished by genocidal attacks, spread of new pathogens (and sometimes intentionally with infected blanket "gifts" for the Natives), and warfare fought by the Lakota to protect their homeland. I hated listening to biased history accounts.

I walked back through the avenue of flags to a gift store. I thought sarcastically, maybe I could keep myself busy shopping for souvenirs. They might have some Native American jewelry. I always tried to buy authentic Indian jewelry that helped support local artisans. The store was almost empty of tourists since most of the visitors were watching the film.

The usual trinkets were everywhere. I saw postcards, and playing cards plastered with the iconic presidential faces. There were coffee mugs and T-shits, sweatshirts, and visors, all stenciled with the park's logo and images. I made my way past the videos and books, toys, and assorted sundries. Finally, I could see a jewelry case in the back. I wandered through the miscellaneous merchandise until I was standing right next to it.

The case was filled with Native American jewelry. A small sign taped on it explained that this collection had been recovered from pawn shops in the area. There were beautiful squash blossom turquoise-and-silver necklaces. There were many inlaid rings and pins with various gemstones, all hand crafted. Many looked very old. The turquoise bracelets caught my attention. There among them was one I thought I recognized. It had two rows of petite turquoise stones, all the exact same size. Could it be? How could that happen? My heart raced, and I ran to find John as quickly as I could.

"John, John, come here please! You won't believe what I found!" I shouted through the noisy people who were streaming out of the amphitheater following the end of the evening program.

"What is it?" he asked as he neared.

"Oh my God, I can't believe it! They have a box of pawned jewelry for sale in the back of the store. I swear to you there is one in there that was once mine! My grandmother gave me a turquoise bracelet when I was in high school. One day, when I was taking it off for gym class, I put it in the locker and turned to untie my shoes. When I went to lock my locker, the bracelet was gone! Someone stole it, right there in the busy locker room at Agoura High School. No one would ever admit it, and there was nothing I could do about it. I know it sounds crazy, but that's the same one! Please come and look. I have to get it back."

"How do you know it's not another one that looks like yours?" he asked.

"I know it's mine. There are two things. First of all, the fourth stone is cracked in half. You will see that when you look in the box. The other thing is that there is a crack in the soldering between the two rows of stones. You can't see that from the top. We will have to ask someone to open the box. If we hold the bracelet up to the light, we will see the crack. I'm sure of it!"

Joe and Alyson came up quickly to hear my news. We all entered and made our way through the store that was busy now with souvenir buyers. We found a shop employee nearby who we quickly enlisted to help us.

The case was unlocked, and I picked up the bracelet. I held it up to the light and there was the crack, just as I had described. Everyone looked astonished.

"We aren't leaving this place until we buy that bracelet, are we?" John asked.

"Oh my God, it's my bracelet. It's been thirty years since I have seen it! I wonder how it got here to South Dakota?" I was in complete awe. "Of course, we have to have it," I stated.

After paying two hundred dollars for my bracelet, I started to cry. I loved it and never thought I would see it again, and here it was, once again, on my arm. I wondered if the spirit world had guided me to this store. I certainly would have never gone to the monument if Joe and Alyson hadn't wanted to see it. I wanted to keep the bracelet on my arm forever. I wish the bracelet could tell me the story of how it had traveled over the thirty-year period from Agoura to South Dakota. It is more than coincidental that I recovered it, and the bracelet has become a symbol to me that the spirit world is real.

BETRAYAL

CHAPTER 23

On September 11th, 2001, with the Twin Towers burning to the ground, America was attacked by terrorists who had flown planes into buildings. The climate of fear and sadness was everywhere. It made me confused, and I questioned my purpose in life. My colleagues and I watched the horror on the television in my school department mailroom. I sat with numb students in the classroom, skipped the normal lessons, and finally went to fulfill my office hours. The phone rang.

"Hello, Francesca?"

"Yes. Oh, hi Christine, what's up? Why are you calling me at work?"

Christine was a former student. Near my age, as a re-entry community college student, we clicked. I liked her sense of humor, her Mexican American pride, and her determination to make her world better by being active politically. When I first met her, she had recently lost her mother to cancer and needed to figure out how to keep their family home. She decided to go back to school and become a grade schoolteacher. Part of her general education was to take an anthropology course. While in my anthropology class, she met her partner, Sean. He was a re-entry student using his G.I. bill to get his education. Sean was quiet but a stellar student. He would tease Christine by taking her favorite seat in the classroom. Their friendship blossomed into romance, and the two have remained my dear friends for decades now. Even as my close friend, it was unusual for her to call me at work.

"You better sit down," she said. "Victor was killed this morning." I immediately thought of the terrorist attacks I had been watching on the news all morning. How could that be? He lived here in California, and I had just seen him a few days earlier, so I knew he was in town.

"He was in a car accident in the Cajon Pass."

We hadn't known Victor for long but respected his determination to succeed at life. He was a Russian immigrant who worked construction. We came to know each other through our mutual friend, Christine, and we spent time together cooking and making tea in his samovar. We laughed and shared stories with his family and mine. I was heartbroken at the loss. It was such a coincidence that he died about the same time as the terrorist attacks happened on the East Coast. Grieving for him, though, would add to our family stress. We were experiencing serious financial problems.

John was having a difficult time with his business. His mail order trade niche, where collectors could buy and sell rare plastic sci-fi model kits, was being eroded by the emergence of eBay.

"What is this new eBay thing all about?" I asked him one day.

"People can now bypass a middleman in the sale of their treasures. They don't need me to find buyers. It's an online auction house that anyone can use," he answered.

At the same time people were paranoid about receiving packages because someone started sending letters laced with anthrax through the mail to newsrooms. Orders slowed down because customers were afraid of being poisoned. With very few sales in months, John decided he would have to close the business he had created with twenty-five years of hard work. Since his business income was a big part of our family finances, we would have to file for bankruptcy. I knew that John was feeling like a failure. Although he was not a practitioner, he was brought up in a Mormon household where men were supposed to take care of their families. He carried a lot of traditional values like this. He was in his forties, and he would have to start a new career. He worried about how he could transition back into the wage-working world after being self-employed. He wasn't even sure about the work he could do. Each day, John sank into deeper depression with the news in the media, the deaths of friends and acquaintances, and the business failure. Our relationship was affected by this. We fought more, and that only added to John's misery.

On that day it was a warm fall afternoon, the kind of Southern California day when the Santa Ana winds dry the field grass crisp. The smell of the leaves, the dust and the pollen lay heavy on our chest, like the burdens we carried, and it made it hard to breathe. Rachael was working hard on her senior thesis for the university. She decided to take a break from her studies to check the pool on the ranch as I had asked her to do. The pool yard was near the little house where John had set up his business. That day John was over there checking on some paperwork.

The front door flew open, and Rachael stomped through, tears streaming down her face. She turned to me in the kitchen and screamed, "Your goddamn husband just propositioned me. What a fucker!" She exploded into heavy, heaving sobbing.

"What?" Did I hear wrong? I was confused and didn't think I had heard her right. "What happened? What are you talking about, Rachael? What is going on?" I shrieked.

Sobbing, she yelled, "Go ask him yourself!"

I ran out of the house to John's office, with thousands of thoughts slicing through my mind. Maybe she misunderstood what he'd said. I knew that John was dedicated to me; he never gave me reason to think that he would want sex with someone else. Oh God! Why would he be seducing my daughter? That was just sick. Tears started flowing uncontrollably, and I felt hurt, angry, sick, dizzy, and weak all at once. I wrapped my arms around myself to keep my insides from coming out.

John was on the front porch, leaning on the white railing as I approached him. His face looked like a stranger's. I had never seen that blank, staring expression before. My heart fell into my stomach, and I knew later I would be throwing it up. I stopped and stared at him, trying to catch my breath. Finally, I asked, "Did you just proposition my daughter for sex?" Words I could have never imagined coming out of my mouth. He had been a dedicated stepfather to my children for the past six years.

"Yes," was all he said.

As I gasped, I squeaked out, "Why?"

What seemed like hours passed. Then he said, "All hell is breaking loose, she looked sexy in the sun with her tank top, and I figured, why not?"

My mouth dropped open, and I just stood there looking at this man I thought I had known who was now so alien to me. I had loved him so entirely, and thought our relationship was perfect and would last forever. It was unbelievable. My body was aching in every way. Help me God, I thought, there isn't enough oxygen in the air, and I could hardly talk.

Gaining some control, I said, "I want you moved out! You

cannot stay at my home with me and my children anymore. You are sick, and I don't want you anywhere near us."

He didn't answer. He just looked down at the ground.

I ran home as fast as I could, adrenaline surging through my veins, and found Rachael still sobbing. I had never known betrayal like this before, and it felt like daggers were being thrust into every part of my soul. I took a deep breath. I started to gain strength with my motherly instincts. I needed to help my daughter feel safe. I told her I would not let John in the house. I would protect her, my first born. I held her, and we cried and cried in the heat of the day.

ALONE AGAIN, NATURALLY

CHAPTER 24

I thought I had known John well, and I thought that we had a good relationship. Maybe I had ignored the red flags of danger I had witnessed until it was too late. Maybe that time he was depressed and didn't want to go to my brother's wedding was a sign. Maybe his lack of interest in socializing with my friends meant something. Any odd and anti-social behavior I had seen in John over the years came back to my memory. All these augmented by the fact that our relationship had had a rocky start. When all these things had happened, I had just rationalized them away. I assumed it was because he was having a bad day, and his attitude had nothing to do with me or our relationship. Now I thought it must have been more than that. Maybe he even regretted that he had chosen to have a relationship with me, and he was suppressing the thoughts in himself. My mind kept ruminating about our years together, and it was getting me nowhere because this was so out of character for him. It must have been that John was having a midlife crisis. I tried to sympathize, but I felt so betrayed.

John and I separated. He told me that he would go to a counselor to discuss what happened. The lonely days at the house seem to go on and on. I went to work, took care of my children, and thought incessantly about it all. I missed John, but the old one, not the one who had betrayed me.

After a few weeks of his personal counseling, he asked me if we could go to another counselor together to discuss what happened. I agreed. The therapist was a woman, probably in her late sixties. Her gray hair and lined face told me she had had plenty of experience with situations like these. Her calm demeanor was constant and cool as she asked us questions and allowed us to talk. She wanted us to do activities together in the sessions. I was reluctant to play "games" and was bothered that we had to do this. In one, there was an imaginary scenario posed where we were on a sinking ship. Each of us could grab ten items to take to the nearby deserted island. We were both given a list and asked to check off the ten things on it that we would grab to take with us. I completed my list and John completed his. Then we compared lists. I was surprised at how different they were. Then it hit me. I suddenly saw how together we were an amazing team, with different skill sets and ways of thinking. Our combined mindset would have saved our lives in this game. If there was a turning point in my thinking, this was it. This game probably saved our marriage. Eventually, through more weeks of sessions, I gained greater insight. It seemed like John was going through a kind of midlife crisis, maybe even feeling emasculated by losing his ability to be the breadwinner of the house, as I had imagined. He had lost his business and income. John grew up in a dysfunctional family, too. It was hard for him to articulate and even identify his emotions. He never had any positive role models for situations like these. Understanding came, but forgiveness was elusive.

Rachael finished her bachelor's degree and moved away to graduate school. Almost a year passed. John was living in the small house that was his office, and I was starting to miss him more and more. We spoke to each other regularly, and he would often help care for Rebecca. I remembered that I adored sleeping with his warm body. He used to snuggle up with me and wrap his strong arms around me. It always made me feel so safe, feminine, and desirable. I was terrified of sharing my bed with him again, though. I wasn't sure I wanted to ever have sex with him again. I was still wounded and couldn't help thinking about him having desired my daughter.

I worried about how this separation would affect Rebecca. John had been a great father to her, and even though he saw her regularly, I know she missed him being in the house with us. It was all so confusing, and I still wasn't sure what to do in the long run. I knew our relationship was never going to be the same. I mulled everything over and over in my mind continually, every happy and hurtful experience we had ever had. Sometimes I felt like things would get better, most of the time I ached and believed the love John had supposedly felt for me in the past was an illusion that I had created. I told myself if that was the case, everything made sense. I could not believe that John would hurt me so deeply otherwise. When I thought like that, my pain was nearly unbearable.

Weeks and weeks went by, and my routine life felt empty. I would go to work, and I would come home. I was depressed and worried. As much as I wanted to give Rebecca a healthy, stress-free childhood, my separation from John must have affected her as well. Then, I received more bad news.

THE "C" WORD

CHAPTER 25

I got the call from my doctor while I was working at the college during my office hours. "Invasive cancer," was all I heard. The words caused my heart to jump, to beat double time, and if I hadn't been sitting down, I might have fainted. That was the dreaded "C" word that everybody fears to hear. I couldn't believe it was happening to me, especially while I had all this other stress in my life. I turned my thoughts to being practical. Having John living in the house next door took on new meaning. I would need his help, at least with Rebecca. My four-year-old daughter needed her daddy and her mommy. I wouldn't let cancer beat me. I had been waiting several days for the news about the biopsy that I recently had done. The doctor said, "The cancer extends beyond the margins of the biopsy." He explained that it meant there was still cancer inside me. I tried to envision what the cells looked like. Could I see the cancer cells if I looked? I didn't want cancer cells in me. Thinking about all this just made me feel worse. I felt like I was poisoned or infested with parasites. I wanted to purge it or shake it out of me. I didn't understand how my own cells could go rogue.

I was scheduled for immediate surgery. The form of cancer I had was not typical. It was an aggressive form of cervical cancer in the glandular tissue, and they needed to move fast. My friends and family were kind and supportive. They all got together and created a care team to alternate taking care of me and my daughter after my hospital stay. They helped me keep up with my usual chores on the ranch, such as collecting eggs, caring for pets, picking vegetables in the garden, and watering the house plants. Luckily, summer vacation for the school would begin the day of my surgery. Letting John back into my life to help me more made sense. I needed him to drive me to the surgery and help care for me as well.

At this point in my life, I was a regular participant in the local Native American community. The spiritual leader of our group, Robertjohn, was supportive when he heard the news. He suggested I come to a healing ceremony on the Big Pine Reservation, in the Owens Valley, the weekend before my hospital stay. I didn't know what this traditional healing ceremony could offer me, but I decided to go anyway. I thought that I had nothing to lose, and I would take advantage of any kind of healing I could get.

The weekend before my surgery, I drove the long, lonely road through the desert and traveled north along the east side of the Sierra Nevada mountains. There was still plenty of snow on the ridges and peaks, and the valley was starting to brown from the early summer heat. As I arrived at my destination, I saw many participants I knew and felt I would be comfortable there. I would be there for four days. Each day there were many rituals, multiple sweat lodge ceremonies, herbal drinks to consume, medicinal mud applications, and sage smudging for cleansing. The elders and medicine people said prayers over me with eagle wings brushing across my body, sweeping the evil spirits away. At night, all the people shared their stories around a bonfire talking circle. When the long weekend was over, I left with immense mental strength. Even though, with my scientific thinking, I couldn't think of how these activities would be of any use, something unexplainable happened. The experience had a strong positive psychological effect on me. I felt positive. I was ready for my surgery with the conviction that everything would be fine.

Still, the day of my surgery, I didn't want to do it. I knew I had to go through it, though. I knew I had competent surgeons and staff, but I also knew anything could happen when I was under anesthesia. John drove me to the hospital. He assisted me through the check-in procedures. As I was prepped, I relaxed and put my life into the hands of the surgical team. John kissed my forehead and left. I was alone. The many procedures I experienced after that are all blurred together. I remember, though, upon waking from the surgery, that I was in excruciating pain. John was there with a worried look and took my hand. Tears started to flow, and I had hot flashes. I started shaking and I was scared. A compete hysterectomy was performed, and I had a long, stapled incision down my belly. It was going to take at least six weeks to heal and get my strength back. I looked up at John and I knew he was scared, too.

A few days later, while I was still in the hospital, the main surgeon visited me with news from the pathology report. She told me there was no cancer found in the tissue taken from my body. I remembered the other doctor telling me the cancer had extended beyond the margins of my biopsy. I wondered how it could be that no cancer was later found. Maybe the biopsy was wrong, or at the cancer was right at the margin. Maybe something else had happened. As a scientist, I am aware of the power of psychological effect. I wondered if my mind had healed my body. I had wondered if the spirit world would come to my aid at the healing ceremony. I didn't know why the cancer was gone, when it supposedly had been there after the biopsy. It didn't matter to me though; it was gone. I thought of John. Maybe my cancer was a metaphor for my relationship with John. The cells in my body had gone rogue, and the recovery happened with the combination of spiritual and scientific healing. Maybe our relationship could be healed, too.

After I returned from the hospital, I slowly gained my strength. Since John decided to be there to help me at the house, my relationship with him improved. He was concerned and attentive. He cared for Rebecca and waited on my every need. As I gained strength, we continued to go to marriage counseling. I began to think the relationship could be salvaged. Of course, I was still hurt by his betrayal, and he was still living in the small back house, but with his care and nurturing after the surgery, I remembered the old John and felt optimistic. He really did love me. Most importantly, he told me he was sorry. The words didn't magically make everything better, but they helped. We talked about him moving back to the house, and one day, I finally agreed. I was scared, but deep inside I only wanted to do what was right and best for my child.

NOTHING LASTS FOREVER

CHAPTER 26

I grew stronger again. During my recovery, I had my constant companion, Milo, near my side. As I moved from room to room, he followed. My favorite marmalade tabby slowly rubbed against my legs. He needed help getting on my lap now, in his old age. He was almost twenty and suffering from diabetes, arthritis, and who knows what else. He'd slowed down so much in the last few months; I knew he wouldn't live much longer. He was once a thriving marmalade twenty-five-pound ball of fur. By this time, he didn't even weigh ten pounds. I lifted him gently, and he purred instantly as he snuggled on my warm lap. I loved this cat so much and had had him through so many changes in my life.

After he jumped off, I noticed there was a whisker on my lap.

"Whoo hoo, another whisker!" I said, pleased about getting to tell John.

I have a collection of cat whiskers. It's not as though I go around and snip off whiskers from random cats or anything like that. Cats shed their whiskers like we shed our hair, and when I find them, like the one Milo had left on my lap, I put them in a tin mint container. I have been doing this for decades and I probably have a whisker from each of the twenty-some-odd cats I have owned during that span of time. I thought, if scientists ever develop methods for cloning cats from retrieved DNA found on whiskers, then I can bring back some of my favorite cats. I have always had more than one cat, though, and it was impossible to tell who had lost their whisker on any particular day. I laughed when I thought about how, with my luck, I might end up cloning one of my neurotic rescue cats. I don't collect whiskers with the dream of cloning them, though. I just keep them as a memento of the love that the cats shared with me. I thought maybe I should mark this one, so I know it's Milo's. I was happy to know that for sure I now had one from him.

Most people adopt cats. They go to a shelter, or a pet store, and find the cat they want and bring it home. That never happens to me. My cats adopt me. Milo adopted me when I was living at the family student housing with my kids at UCR. After we returned from my field research in Spain, I had new neighbors, Lisa and Randy. They had an orange female who ended up birthing two huge orange kittens before they were able to get her spayed. Because we are cat lovers, my kids and I visited the kittens regularly and stroked their fat, silky bodies. They got older and ventured outside and one of them the owners had named Milo. This guy would walk right into my home when the door that was ajar for Bebe, my cat. Bebe tolerated the kitten, mostly ignoring the new intruder. Often, I would come into the living room and find him rolled up, sleeping on my couch. He was so friendly and purred when he saw me. He loved sitting on my lap, too. So, finding him in my house was not a problem; in fact, I loved finding him there.

When I finished writing my dissertation and needed to move from student housing, I moved with Steve to the house, which is now part of my ranch. The new rental place was in a neighborhood near the university. Packing boxes to move to my new house, I knew I would miss my daily visitor, Milo.

On moving day, as I lifted the last box into the truck, I walked over to the neighbors' house to say goodbye. I had already hugged

Randy and Lisa, but Lisa disappeared when I turned around. Immediately, she came walking out with Milo in her arms. I would get one more cuddle with my friend before I left, I thought.

"Just take him with you. He only loves you anyway," she said.

"Oh my God, Lisa. I couldn't do that to you. I really love Milo so much. I want to take him, but he's your cat."

"We can't have three cats. We have another family lined up to take his brother, so you might as well take Milo. He wouldn't be happy anywhere else."

With tears in my eyes, I put Milo in the car and hugged Lisa again. As I drove to the new house with him sitting calmly on the passenger seat looking up at me with trusting eyes, I knew he would be like no other cat I had ever owned.

When John and I first dated, I had had Milo for a couple years. Milo seemed to be jealous of John. As things heated up between us, and John slipped out of his clothes and into my bed, he made the mistake of leaving his clothes on the floor. Every time he did that, Milo made sure he peed on them. Fortunately, John was a cat lover, and although that behavior made him angry, he knew I loved cats. I knew deep down that he was fond of Milo despite that. Eventually, John learned not to leave clothes on the floor. Milo learned to love John. John had a rough rub with his big hands that only he could do, which I know Milo appreciated. John liked when Milo would sit on his lap and purr.

He grew to be the biggest cat I had ever seen. Through our various life events, Milo was part of the family. After I became John's bride, Milo was there. He kept me happy when I was pregnant, purring on top of my mountain-sized belly. When I was nursing baby Rebecca, he insisted that he sit on my lap at the same time. Rebecca's hands would reach back and finger his fur. I can't help thinking that the familiarity of the sound of purring was what helped her grow up to have a great love of cats. Through the years, Milo was a part of it all: the time I spent part-time teaching, after defending my dissertation and graduating with my Ph.D.; when I got my career full-time teaching position; through good health and during the recovering weeks in bed with various ailments, he was always by my side. Every night he slept by my side. His soul was deeply connected to mine.

I remembered it all as I held his whisker in my hand. I laughed thinking how collecting them was a really odd thing to do. Not a normal collection. Maybe it allows me to hang on to my cats forever? Like so many times in my life though, I felt like the ones I love so intensely eventually abandon me. Not even Milo could live forever.

Soon after I had saved this whisker, Milo died at age twenty. We buried him under the citrus trees on the ranch. Grief was becoming a normal feeling for me. Each loss in life that you experience is equally painful, though. Of course, I have experienced plenty of loss, from pets to people. Each loss leaves a void nothing else can fill.

Painting of Milo by Rachael

RITE OF PASSAGE

CHAPTER 27

Rebecca insisted on being called Ray now. If Rebecca had been male at birth, we would have named her Raymond after John's grandfather. Rebecca started to identify as male, so it seemed logical to her to adopt that name. I reluctantly agreed to use the name. I realized it was harmless. I remember being called "Frankie" in high school. Sometimes using a nickname gives you a sense of individuality. I wasn't ready for more changes, though.

Ray wanted to cut her hair. This thought really upset me. Ray had gorgeous, thick, waist-length blond hair. It shined like gold in the sun. Also, she was able to grow her hair so easily, and it was the kind of hair that I dreamed of having. Ever since she was a tiny toddler, I would braid her hair every morning in a routine. She hated it when I would brush out tangles, but it became a ritual time for us to connect. We would talk about what was going to happen in school that day, or what weekend activities were coming up. I thought of this time as a mother-daughter bonding experience. Cutting off her hair would end this special time. Ray hated the hair because it looked so feminine, and she was trying to look more masculine. She was wearing boy clothes now and stuffing her braid up in hats when she could.

"I hate my hair. It's heavy, hard to wash. I'm going to cut it off," she said defiantly one day.

"No, don't do that!" I begged. "I love your hair. Hair is power." I always said that to make her feel proud of long hair. I came from the generation of long-haired hippie types, and I had been spending more time interacting in the Native American community. Long hair was always seen as beautiful and something to be proud of.

"You can't stop me, and I'm just going to do it. I won't look like a girl so much with short hair," Ray said.

I knew she would just do it whether I liked it or not. How could I stop her? "Oh my god, let me cut it then. I don't want you to botch it up." I acquiesced. "Let's plan to do it tomorrow afternoon." I figured that would give me time to start to get used to the idea.

I called my friend and colleague Lynda to tell her what was going to happen. Lynda was a professor of Health and Human Sexuality in the biology department where I taught. I remember walking across campus when I first started working there and people saying, "Hi Lynda!" I wondered who that "Lynda" was and realized it was Lynda in my department. We looked similar. We both were tall, had long, dark hair with bangs, and wore long earrings. She and I instantly became friends. We bonded when we discovered that we both had a lot in common, like having issues with our mothers and being old hippie types who loved men and being sexy. She was a few years older than me, so I thought of her as a big sister. She had a lot of life wisdom, and with her academic knowledge of sexuality as well, there were plenty of fun things to talk about regarding men. We went out to lunch regularly and teamed up at department meetings. She hated the meetings as much as I did, and we did silly things like asking the Magic 8 Ball that we had hidden under the table questions about Lynda's hot dates or my mundane married life. She even came to pow wows with me, the Native American gatherings in our community, and we danced together during intertribal dances. We shared a lot of laughs, but worked hard together, too. We developed and co-taught a class in cross-cultural human sexuality, combining her human sexuality expertise and my anthropology expertise. She was my work BFF. When Ray started questioning her gender identity, Lynda was a trusted source of information and moral support.

"I'll come over and be there, if you want," she told me on the phone. I was relieved that she had suggested that.

The next day was beautiful. It was sunny and warm, and Ray was ready to rid herself of the hair. Lynda arrived, and I told Ray that she was going to help me. I was already choked up and saddened by the deed I was about to do. I was grateful Lynda had come over.

We went out to the front yard lawn. In the warmth of the sun, I started by braiding the golden tresses and stroking them for the last time. I thought about all the years of my motherly love embedded in them, by brushing, braiding, and nurturing it all. I felt tears welling up in my eyes. Ray looked joyous and could hardly sit still. This was a day she had been looking forward to as much as I had been dreading it.

"Cut it off!" she said without any doubt in her voice. She knew what she wanted.

I looked at Lynda. She was smiling, and she nodded. She knew this was something Ray needed to do. I started crying. Before I totally broke down, I took the scissors and lopped off the braid. Ray was free! I held the limp braid like a tether to the past that had fallen apart. I never wanted to let go of this treasure. I felt transformed though. There was no turning back now. Ray was male in my mind now and Rebecca was gone. My little girl just vanished into history. I remembered the stuffed animals she had cuddled like babies and the dress-up wardrobe of Disney princess gowns and tiaras. I was sobbing hard now; I had to sit down. Ray danced around the yard laughing. He was transformed as well.

"I can't cut any more. I'll have to take you to get it styled in a boy cut." I barely could say these words. "My stylist, Jennifer, could help with that, I'm sure," Lynda said. She patted my shoulder to reassure me, and we both knew it was the right thing to do.

RITE OF PASSAGE

I held her long braid
In my hands.
"Chop it off!"
She said firmly,
"It's not who I am anymore."
So much effort to wash,
Brush and carry that hair.
She hated it.
I loved it.
The daily ritual
Of motherly care,
Lovingly combing,
And plaiting the golden strands.
So much had changed
Over the years,
Embedded in the inches.
But, no more.
I cried
And cried and I cut,
To free her from her childhood.

JUNGLE MISHAPS AND THE HEART GROWS FONDER

CHAPTER 28

Time is a tricky thing. It seems like events happen, and then when you talk about them in the past tense like they were only in the recent past, you'll find that in reality a lot of time has gone by. I am always shocked when I look at Facebook memories. I see a photo I posted five years ago and think it has only been a year or two at most since I posted it.

John and I had to deal with our child's gender change, and I was impressed with his sensible, caring way of dealing with the situation I talked about in the opening of this book. Rebecca was now Ray, and we were adapting. John and I were still working on strengthening our relationship, as well.

It was Valentine's Day, and I managed to drag myself to school and back. I left the heart-shaped candy boxes with cards for John and Ray on the kitchen counter in the morning. After work, I walked in the front door and saw a new box with John's familiar writing on an envelope. I was relieved that he had come through and happy to have some chocolates of my own. It's these little things that make my heart skip a beat and that remind me of the romance in the relationship that my husband and I once had.

I opened the envelope with my name carefully scripted and saw a folded piece of computer paper. As I pulled it out, I saw a photo from the internet with a zoo jaguar licking a pink, heart-shaped piece of ice. Inside, John had written, "Ready to go see the jaguars in Brazil?" Oh Wow. I squealed and jumped up and down and thought, "Oh my God, I am so ready."

It was my dream since I was a teenager to go to the Amazon jungle, but I didn't know about the other natural areas of Brazil until later. I had learned about these jaguars from a colleague at school, Sherry, who had taken a photographers' tour of the Pantanal region to see them. Because I was a cat fan, I knew that trip had to be in my future. I remember talking about it for days after seeing Sherry's photos. I told John that I wanted to do that kind of trip one day, but I never imagined it would happen so soon. The Valentine's gift was a gesture of love, and I was happy to feel another twinge of affection. John had arranged an almost three-week excursion to Brazil. We'd spend most of our time looking at jaguars, capybaras, caimans, monkeys, and any other wildlife we could see. Then we would spend several days on a boat in the Amazon jungle. All my life I have wanted to go to the mighty Amazon jungle. I could hardly wait for the journey.

Finally, it was summer vacation, and we went. It was a long day of travel and even though our adrenalin was high with the thought of adventure, we were exhausted. John's friend Rob joined us for the adventure, and Ray was traveling with his new male passport for the first time. We arrived in Brasilia and had to get our luggage before going through customs and catching a domestic flight to Cuiabá. We congregated at the baggage claim carousel and waited and waited. And waited. Everyone was nervous.

"I hope we don't miss our next flight." I was agitated but felt I needed to say this to John. His perturbed expression told me he was feeling the same way.

Just as he was going to speak, an airline representative arrived and spoke very loudly. His accent was thick, and I could hardly understand him.

"He says the bags are not arriving. They have all been sent to Rio de Janeiro," a nearby fellow passenger told us. The summer Olympics were beginning, and in the confusion, our bags had accidently been diverted there. There was grumbling and a bit of confusion following this news. Oh great, I thought. My anxiety was already pumped up, and with this news, my heartbeat increased more.

John quickly figured out what we needed to do for customs and filled out some forms. Soon we boarded the next flight without any luggage other than our carry-on bags.

"I hope they arrive before we head out into the jungle," I said. I couldn't believe this was happening to us. Tapping my finger on the arm rest of the seat, I shot a glance at John. He shook his head and muttered something under his breath.

At Cuiaba, we met our tour operator and explained the situation. He assured us that he would come back for the bags when they arrived. He drove us to a hotel for the evening. We had no way of knowing what would happen. What if our luggage never came? We decided we should try and buy some essential things. Rob and John set out on a walk down the street to a supermarket to try and buy some basic needs, like toothbrushes and socks. I went through my carry-on bag to see what I could share. John, Rob, and Ray all had electronics and cameras in their carry-on bags. I was the only one with extra clothing. I decided that I could share two long-sleeved, button-up shirts, two T-shirts, and some socks. When the guys returned, we sorted everything out. "Which one of you guys wants to wear my pink shirt?" I teased.

The next morning, there was no news of our luggage, and we headed out on our journey and boarded our boat to the remote jaguar reserve. We would have to wash our few clothes out in the night and hope they would dry enough for the next day. We were in the tropics, and the steamy air was heavy with humidity and things took forever to dry. We had no other choice, though.

The days flew by. Everyone was a good sport about wearing my clothes. Fortunately, the daytime excursions and wildlife viewing were spectacular. We barely noticed who was wearing what and the general lack of clean clothes. The towering flowering trees and the bird calls, unrecognizable to me and even John, who was now a wildlife biologist and expert back home, were all around us. Our guides did their best to identity things, and we were absorbed in the lessons. We saw close-ups of the endless docile caimans on the shores and swimming in the river. We saw the comical capybaras who looked like giant guinea pigs that I had kept as pets when I was young. I saw sleeping howler monkeys and foraging spider monkeys. We observed the playful giant river otters. Their heads poking up from the river looked like children's heads. They were fascinating, and I kept wanting to anthropomorphize them. The most wonderful views were of the majestic jaguars lounging on the shores, as we glided by in our small boats. I saw an old jaguar with dull colors and scarred fur, who was obviously used to the small motorboats of tourists going by and wondered if this was such a good fate for these animals. It seemed like this was a zoo on a grand scale. Before tourism was established, farmers would regularly kill these animals for attacking their livestock, as the farmers had expanded further into the jaguars' territory. This "zoo" seemed like a better alternative for them than getting killed and being pushed out of existence.

I got used to seeing my shared clothes on others, and we all smelled about the same. Even though we washed out the clothes by hand in the evenings, they didn't dry by morning, as predicted. I couldn't decide if it was the mildew or the clinging sweat smell that was stronger. After a week in the jungle, we received news that our bags had arrived. We were so thrilled, and after we showered and changed into fresh clothing, we all breathed easier.

Just as we finished our time in the Pantanal, bad luck struck again. Rob got a message from his wife that a doctor's visit had brought her bad news. She had been diagnosed with cancer and needed surgery immediately. Rob arranged for an early departure, and we wished them a successful outcome. We continued our journey and boarded our flight to Manaus.

On the flight, I felt a pain in my lower abdomen. I got queasy and felt faint. "John, I don't feel too good. I'm having severe pain on my right side, here." I pointed to the place on my lower belly. "I think I'm going to throw up. Please help me to the toilet."

John held me up and escorted me to the front of the plane. I got inside the bathroom and vomited. I collapsed on the floor and couldn't stand up because of the pain. I heard John talking to the flight attendant. "My wife is really sick and in a lot of pain," he said.

"John, I can't get up!" I said loudly. He opened the door and helped me up. I was in so much pain, I buckled over. "I need to lie down, please." I was so frightened. I thought that I was having an appendicitis attack. We were high in the sky, and I remembered that I could die if my appendix did break.

The flight attendant cleared an area for me in the front of the plane to lie down. I started to faint, and I was barely conscious when I heard the announcement asking if there was a doctor on the flight. Fortunately for me, there was one. Time was burred as I came in and out of consciousness. The doctor gave me an injection for pain and asked me questions I could barely answer. I realized he was speaking English. John held my hand tightly, and I knew he was worried, and he could tell I was afraid, too. Eventually, I was helped back to my seat while we landed in Manaus. There was an emergency medical team waiting for me when we landed.

The flight attendants spoke in English and Portuguese. "Due to an ill passenger, we ask that you remain in your seats when we arrive at the gate to allow emergency crews to help. Thank you for your cooperation."

With my head spinning from painkillers, I was helped off the plane first, with John and Ray following. I rode a wheelchair in a blur to an airport medical facility. After a quick examination, the doctor at this facility was concerned that I had appendicitis as well. I needed to get to a hospital immediately for a CAT scan. Our new tour guide had connected with us somehow and volunteered to drive us to the nearest hospital.

I was so drugged with painkillers at this point, all I saw were blurs of colors, and all I heard were muffled sounds. I closed my eyes for what felt like a quick drive across Manaus to a hospital emergency room. Things seemed to move quickly, and I was soon being CAT scanned. The doctor and nurses were talking to John through our tour guide interpreter.

As I waited for the news in another room, I was barely conscious. Soon I woke up a little and heard some conversation. "The doctor says that your wife has a kidney stone. He will give her some medicine that will help relax her ureter, so she can pass the stone," the interpreter told my husband. The nurse was busy connecting an IV drip to help hydrate me.

"Can he give her something for the pain as well?" John asked. I rolled and gasped in agony. The other medicine I had received on the plane had worn off.

"Yes. He is getting the prescriptions ready now. We will watch her for a bit to see if she improves."

After a few hours and several trips to the toilet, I felt better. Although I was dizzy from the prescriptions, the stabbing pain on my side had subsided. The doctor allowed us to leave but encouraged me to continue the medicine the next day if I still felt more pain.

We drove to the boat dock, and John assisted me to our cabin. I fell into a deep sleep and woke in the morning on the Rio Negro in the Amazon jungle. By the next day, I had started to feel completely normal. I walked out on the deck and realized that I was in the Amazon jungle.

The trees were thicker and greener than in the Pantanal region. I barely heard the birds above the drone of the boat's motor as we headed deeper into the wilds. At lunch time, the captain directed the small crew to tie the boat up to the shore. The motor was turned off. The cacophony of jungle sounds was music to my ears. It was beautiful because I heard howler monkeys, birds, and things unknown. The pungent smell of sweet flowers and decaying plants in the water was like nothing I had ever known. A large, emerald-colored dragon fly landed near my hand. I felt like I was in a dream. After lunch, we decided to take a smaller boat out to skirt the shores and look for other wildlife.

This became our routine for several days. At night, the crew moved us in a larger boat while we slept, and in the day, we explored in the smaller boat. One day, we went piranha fishing.

John proudly showed off his catch as I photographed him. On another day, we went for a walk through the jungle with a traditional Native healer who showed us the plants that are used for medicines. I was a big fan of Mark Plotkin and his book *Tales of the Shaman's Apprentice*. Mark is an ethnobotanist who studies the traditional use of plants by Native people. I loved reading his stories and had dreamed of being able to walk through a rainforest with a medicine man, as his work required. And here I was! I learned about the bark on trees that can be used for anxiety and fruit pods that can be used as salves on skin cuts. I only wished I had months instead of hours to listen to the translator telling me what the medicine man was saying. John added to his bird list, I felt like the seasoned anthropologist I always wanted to be, and Ray got the opportunity of his life to go where few of his friends would ever go.

Too soon, it was over. I had ticked off another "bucket list" life item, and we returned home from our adventure. Once we were home, I thought about how concerned John had been, so very kind and nurturing throughout the trip, especially when I was sick. I sank into my cozy bed and thought about how glad I was that I had stuck it out through the tough times in our marriage. He really loves me.

ABANDONMENT MAGNET

CHAPTER 29

I have taught thousands of students. Some, I have no memory of at all. Some I remember well, and some have become life-long friends. I love that I can see how each has a unique story of their own, and how sometimes their lives have impacted mine in profound ways.

Wandering between the decorated shops at Olvera Street on Día de Los Muertos, I am looking for a face that I know should be there. Carlos had told me he always comes for this celebration. As a Mexican American, he grew up in East Los Angeles, and going to Olvera Street was an easy getaway where he could enjoy authentic Mexican food, crafts, and candies. This was where he had learned to sing the traditional mariachi ballads that he loved. I pass hordes of laughing and painted faces. The altars are packed with pictures of loved ones who have died, along with their favorite foods, bright orange marigolds, and frosting-decorated sugar skulls. Suddenly, a band blasts their brass, and a tenor sings his songs, bold and passionate. The singer is good. He sounds a bit like Carlos, but it's not him. It is Carlos I am searching for. I miss him and his beautiful singing voice, his laugh, and most importantly, his warm friendship.

We met a few years ago in a class I teach at a local college. I start each semester with an ice-breaking session, so students can learn about each other and feel more comfortable in my discussion activities.

"Hi everyone, my name is Carlos. I was a career Marine for over twenty years, stationed overseas. One day, I got a phone call telling me my seventeen-year-old son, back here in the States, committed suicide."

The younger students were completely still, mouths dropped open, and eyes fixed on Carlos.

"Yeah, that kind of news makes you crazy. Well, I was sent home. I got divorced and ended up homeless, wandering around the streets for two years. It's a good thing my older sister found me in the desert. I was almost dead." He continued nonchalantly, "She brought me back to my mom's. That's why I'm here at school. It's time to retool and make a new life."

With that introduction, I was hooked. Here was a re-entry student in a classroom full of soul-searching young adults, and I wondered, how does one overcome obstacles like those? This guy had something to teach all of us. After class, I invited Carlos to participate in the Native American club where I served as the faculty advisor. He gladly accepted and became an active member.

After a year of events, the other students and I became good friends with Carlos. We were mesmerized by his ability to tell spell-binding stories that would often end up as jokes at our meetings. I was invited to celebrate his mother's birthday, beginning the day singing "Las Mañanitas," a traditional Mexican birthday song, outside her home in the early dawn. I was warmly accepted by his extended family, and it was there that I learned about Carlos' magnificent singing voice.

He was a skilled handyman, and he helped me with some of my projects at home during the summer. He worked tirelessly, repairing my appliances, resurfacing my hardwood floors, and painting my walls. During work, we would talk about our interests, especially baseball, a mutual passion. Dodger Stadium at

Chavez Ravine was the place to be on a summer night, donning our Dodger-blue T-shirts, Dodger dogs in hand.

I wrote heartfelt letters of recommendation for scholarships that helped him transfer successfully to UCLA to finish his bachelor's degree. Even after that transfer, he regularly came to our club events and included me in his family gatherings.

In the late spring, our Native club hosted a barbecue in my oak-wooded back yard. We hung a string of sparkling lights, lit tiny candles, and cooked a Southern California feast on the patio grill. Of course, everyone begged Carlos to sing. Having anticipated the request, with his instrument in hand, he caressed his blond guitar and sang one love song after another, melting my heart as never before. I sensed that our friendship was changing, since he regularly looked over at me with long gazes. I felt confused about this because I didn't know if there was a message in the songs, or maybe in the order he sang them. It occurred to me that maybe he was falling in love with me.

The last text I had gotten from him was on opening day of baseball season at Dodger Stadium. I wrote, "I wish I could go!" and he answered, "Me too." Then oddly, there was nothing. I tried texting, writing email letters, and making phone calls. It was as if he had vanished from the planet. Some friends successfully contacted him, and they told me that he was fine, only busy. I patiently waited, thinking he would eventually get back to me. Months went by. I mulled it over and over in my mind, trying to figure out what had caused the abrupt end to our interaction. Sometimes, I thought that I had offended him. Sometimes, I thought I had overstepped my ethical boundary as his former college professor and let him think I wanted something more than friendship from him. I worried that he was afraid of feelings that he might have been developing for me. I tried not to think it was anything I did and maybe he had just met someone and had fallen in love and was too caught up in the romance to talk to me. I wanted to talk to him, but Carlos never communicated with me again. I was still hoping our paths would cross again, though, because what I knew was that I really cared about him.

Loud drumming and the sounding of the conch shell wake me from my daydream. The Aztec dancers offer the burning copal incense to the four directions and lead the Day of the Dead procession to the plaza for their ritual dancing. I edge my way through the sea of unrecognizable faces, still searching, and veer off to my parked car with the sinking feeling that I have to accept that I will never see Carlos again.

First group of students in the Intertribal Student Alliance - Back L-R: Mohini, Vanessa, Elda, Grace, Laura, and Roxanne. Front L-R: Jason and Brandon (missing Eddie, but not forgotten).

SWEATING TO THE OLDIES

CHAPTER 30

I cleaned the house and cooked dinner, some bread, pozole soup, and berry pies, for thirty people or more. Some others had come early to chop wood, rake the grounds, and prepare the lodge. It was strenuous, time-consuming work, but we don't mind because we have been waiting all month since our last sweat for this day to come. We feel lucky to participate in this ancient Native American rite because it makes us feel renewed, recharged, and ready for more of our tough lives. I know my own healing from and understanding of the trauma I experienced in life often happened while in the sweat lodge. For a few decades now, sweats have helped me cope with life's difficulties.

What I really love is the company of the local Native community, including my friends, students, and sometimes new guests of the regulars. To be the steward of the lodge is a great responsibility. However, I feel fortunate and blessed to have the ceremony take place on my ranch.

My helpers started to show up early in the day as the preparations began. Our spiritual leader, Robertjohn, arrived later to perform his specific tasks. He is our sweat master, the name for someone who officiates the ceremony, or "pours the water." He's a strong and vibrant white-haired man in his eighties who eagerly teaches us all he knows about his knowledge of Native American ways. He's the type of person who never says what you want him to say, but that's how he educates us. He forces people to think. He says things like, "Everything is related, and the earth is mother to all. She is completely nurturing, giving us what we need to survive, and provides unconditional love. Regardless of what we do to her, with pollution, overpopulation, and overexploitation, she continues to nurture us." We all ponder these words.

Despite five hundred years of the colonizing culture's attempt to try and eradicate Native knowledge, this man carries fragments of the past about the ancient ways taught to him by his traditional Paiute and Iroquois elders. He often tells us what his grandfather in the Owens Valley on the east side of the Sierra Nevada mountains and relatives in Canada and New York taught him well. He reminds us that in the Euro/American culture that we live in, we see ourselves as separate from nature, above it, and special. Yet, he was taught that we need to learn to respect our place in the natural order of life, and the sweat lodge ceremony is a ritual in which we spend time reconnecting with our mother, the earth.

I wasn't brought up in the traditional Native American ways, but I came to learn about the sweat lodge ceremony as an adult, when a Native friend brought me to a ceremony decades ago near Wrightwood, California. It has been over thirty years since I first attended, and I have gone regularly ever since. Our local community had a sweat lodge in Upland that I used to attend monthly. The ceremonial ground was in a junkyard next to the Graber Olive House. After several years, the property was sold for development, and we were told to shut down the lodge. We were devastated. Where would the community go? There are so many rules and regulations in the city about open fires, but sacred fires are necessary for ceremony.

Robertjohn's youngest daughter, a pre-teen participant named Kayleen, cried when she learned we would be moving because she loved a huge mulberry tree that was there. The majestic branches held a swing where she regularly played. I was so touched by her tears that I decided to try something. I broke off several branches from the tree and rooted them. When that was successful, I planted them on my ranch. I told myself that if they grew, maybe I was meant to have the new sweat lodge grounds here. Much to my amazement, they flourished. After some time of negotiation with my husband and Robertjohn, it was settled. The new sweat lodge would be at my ranch.

The structure and the function of the lodge are thousands of years old. There is a rigid protocol to its preparation. When making the hut, we collected willow branch poles by a stream. Each was about the diameter of my wrist. Then, at the place we selected, we dug the poles into the ground in a circle shape, like fence posts, and bent them over into a dome. We wove the branches and tied them all together in a prescribed way. Finally, we covered the dome with heavy tarps. We made a doorway, with a flap, facing east. We enter this familiar room for the ceremony in the night, sit on the earth and sing songs, some of which are older than recorded time. Each ceremony is conducted with the same attention to detail. Although strictness of tradition is necessary, at times Robertjohn adds something new that makes each ritual experience unique.

Today, when the helpers began to clean the lodge, I thought about how much the ranch has changed over the years. The Black Widow Ranch got its name when my husband John and I bought the property over a decade ago. It was a run-down, trash-filled, ex-horse ranch. All the old buildings, barrels, tires, and decomposing lumber were the perfect habitat for these venomous spiders. After years of clean-up, and rehabilitation of the property by planting thousands of native trees and plants, we are in control of the situation, but the name persists. We secretly enjoy the perplexed reactions we get from people when they learn the name, and joke that black widows are the only thing that we can successfully raise here. Our ranch is in a semi-desert environment, filled with the native scrub plants we had reintroduced. There is a pond area that is tranquil and lush with tall willows, cottonwoods, and sycamores, surrounding the lily-filled water. Coyotes, bobcats, skunks, raccoons, foxes, squirrels, rabbits, and birds now find the ranch a safe refuge on the edge of the city of Riverside. We built the sweat lodge in the center of some trees, near the pond, concealing it from curious people who might drive by the property.

A first timer, who had shown up early to help, introduced himself to Robertjohn. He handed him a small bundle of sage. "I'm pretty nervous about this," he said. "I've always wanted to go to a sweat ceremony but never had the chance. Thanks for letting me come today. What will happen?" Robertjohn told him, "We will go into the lodge to let the spirit world work." I thought about how it's a time for prayer, contemplation, and meditation. As an aside, Robertjohn continued, "In the old days, there was no Native American word for prayer. We were told to just 'do our talking.'" I thought about how there is so much we could tell this new person, but the best way to understand is to just experience it.

Robertjohn taught us the sweat lodge is as the womb of Mother Earth, and after a time inside, participants emerge from the lodge reborn. In a sense, it is a Native American church, but more. In my anthropological understanding, I see how Christian philosophy came to use this metaphor of rebirth for when one becomes

Christian and is "born again." Indigenous peoples all over the world practiced the sweat lodge ceremony for thousands of years, and the ceremony surely predates Christianity. It is also clear that this ritual is beneficial to the participants. I know that the altered state of consciousness that one achieves, due to the heat, darkness and hypnotic, rhythmic songs, affects the functioning of the brain to allow one to rethink and solve problems in different and new ways. When one leaves the lodge, they feel renewed.

Meanwhile, while Robertjohn talked to the newcomer, the other helpers removed the rocks that were inside the lodge from the previous ritual so that they could be reheated. The ground inside the lodge was smoothed, and they smudged everything with the smoke of a dried bundle of sage. This "spiritual soap," as I like to call it, is like incense and is used to remove any lingering bad spirits. Outside the lodge, other helpers created a medicine wheel, a circle with a cross in it, of tobacco in the fireplace. They bowed their heads in prayer and prepared for the fire. They laid down wood, arranged a pyramid of rocks in the center, and covered the rocks with kindling and wood. I am aware that other tasks are done that I'm not privy to know. When all was set up, I was asked to light the fire. After I gave my tobacco offering with a prayer, I lit the fire.

Our rocks are called "the ancient ones" or "the grandfathers" because they were here first, eons before any of us. We have some of the same minerals in our bodies that are in those rocks, and thus we are connected, related. The fire around the rocks must burn for at least two hours, sometimes more if the weather is cool, to heat them properly. So, we wait. When the time comes, the grandfathers are glowing red.

Unlike other places where I have participated in sweat

ceremonies, Robertjohn likes to have a “talking circle” before we go into the lodge. He says that by doing this we can introduce ourselves to everyone and state why we have come to sweat. It also helps us get all our chatting out, so when we go into the lodge, we can focus and “do our talking,” and we don’t feel like we have to whisper to each other.

We formed a circle, and after we smudged with sage to remove any negative spirits, one by one, we took turns speaking. Robertjohn spoke last. He addressed any major topics that were spoken about, healing us in a Jungian way, and recited some basic protocol. We were reminded, and mostly for the benefit of the new people, to make sure we had relieved ourselves of bodily pressures, to ask permission to enter the lodge, and to recall that only one person was to speak at a time.

With a signal from Robertjohn, we put on our sweat clothes at the appropriate dressing areas. The women went to the house, the men went behind clumps of trees. The women wear long, loose dresses that are modest, like Hawaiian muumuus, and the men wear swim trunks. We gathered with our towels at the lodge door and were smudged with sage once more before we went in. We took turns and individually offered a bit of tobacco to the fire with a prayer of our intentions. We told the spirit world why we had come and what we hoped to get out of the experience.

Like most Native sweat lodge ceremonies, this ritual occurs in “rounds.” Each round, or portion of the ceremony, is symbolic of a particular stage of life. As we proceed through the ritual, we experience the life cycle, reflecting on a particular phase of our life and the experiences we have had in the past, or envisioning the life we hope to have in those future phases. It is, therefore, a therapeutic pursuit to become the best human being one can possibly become through introspection.

Robertjohn had already entered the lodge alone. He did his duties and prayers that were only between him and the spirit world. A door man then bowed to the earth and entered next, to sit by the door, close and open the flap, and help bring in rocks as needed. All other participants then got down on their hands and knees one by one, and asked permission to enter the lodge. The older women went in first, the group that I was with, followed by the younger women, and lastly the men. As we entered, we all said, "All my relations!" in our native language or English to announce to the spiritual and natural world that we were there, and that we affirmed our connection to all.

When everyone was in place, the men on the south side of the lodge and the women on the north side, sitting with our backs against the tent walls, Robertjohn asked for six rocks to be brought into the lodge and placed them in a hole in the center of the floor, one at a time. These rocks represent the universe, one for each cardinal direction, north, south, east, west, plus one for above and one for below. Robertjohn was creating the center of the universe. Special medicinal herbs were sprinkled on the six rocks. The herbs hitting the hot rocks sparkled like little fireflies in the dark lodge. It became smoky and smelled of cedar and sage and other unrecognizable plants. We were told to bless ourselves. We did that by pulling the smoke toward us with our hands and patting our bodies in places where we needed healing. Some who were lonely and sad patted their hearts. Some who were confused or frustrated about a problem patted their heads. I patted my whole body because the older I get, the more I hurt from head to toe.

Those who were outside and had chosen not to participate in the ceremony came near the door along with the fire keepers who tended the rocks. Joining all inside, before the door was closed, we sang two songs to thank the plants and the animals for all they do and to let them know that we have not forgotten them. This is not a traditional practice, but one Robertjohn adopted because he feels it is very important. With a word from Robertjohn, about a quarter of the rocks that are heated were brought in, one by one on a pitchfork. The fire keepers alternated between freezing in the night air and sweating close to the flames. The rocks were pulled from the embers and brushed off with a whiskbroom to ensure that no bits of charcoal were stuck to them because that would bring smoke into the lodge. The door man arranged them on the pile in the center of the lodge using deer antlers like tongs.

When the rocks needed for the first round were in place, the fire keepers carried in a heavy bucket of water. Robertjohn prayed over the water, and the door of the lodge was closed. It was so dark that you couldn't see your hand in front of your face. I sensed the tension and anxiety from the first-timer, but I was eager to begin. Robertjohn said an opening prayer and began to ladle the water onto the rocks. It suddenly became steamy hot. I knew that the first round would be a gentle one since there were children present and they would often only stay for this part. He said, "If it gets too hot for you, lie on the floor. The ground is always cool in the night. Our mother, the earth, is always compassionate and will help us." Sometimes when I lie down, I relax the same way I do when I settle in a hot bath, so I doze off. I was so tired from the day of hard work and found the warm embrace of the lodge completely comfortable. I started to get drowsy, so I sat up. I knew that I was not the only one since I occasionally heard snoring. This, however, was only the beginning of the first round.

The first round is analogous to the stage of life called infancy and early childhood. Robertjohn said that as a baby we are egocentric and concerned only with our own needs. All we want as a baby is to be fed and kept safe and warm. Therefore, like a baby, we are told to be selfish and to pray for ourselves. We prayed to heal our wounds, both physical and psychological. We grieved for the loss of our innocence. It was the only time of the ceremony when we did this. During the round we sang four songs. After that, the sweat lodge door was opened, and cool air rushed in. Many of us saw the steam escaping. Robertjohn told us the clouds of steam are the visible form of the spirits of our ancestors and our spirit helpers, who had come to assist us.

Between the rounds, people asked questions, and in keeping with the formal ritual always asked for permission to speak first. They spoke about their issues or experiences that they were thinking about. People shared their personal relationships, their psychological problems, and their losses. We never discuss these things outside the lodge, as they are revealed to us in confidence. Sometimes Robertjohn gave members advice, at other times, he would recite an ancient parable or talk about science and nature. Other teachings came from personal stories Robertjohn shared about his relationship with his grandfather. I thought about how the experience was a sort of Native American group therapy. I found all the advice to be personally helpful, and over the years. I've resolved many issues in my own life, thought of new things, and learned a lot about love through this activity. I've learned that pain is a teacher, and when we try to ignore our pain, or cover it up, or numb it with alcohol or other chemical substances, we "go to sleep." The lesson that pain wants us to know cannot be learned. In that case, one continues to experience pain. This helped me understand the battle my mother fought and lost as an alcoholic while I was growing up. Meanwhile, as people talked, our sweat master asked the fire keepers to bring another set of rocks into the lodge for the second round.

This round represents maturity, which occurs when our family and good friends become important to us. As our circle of relations grows, we pray for these loved ones. We were taught that one cannot simply pray for a specific person unless they've asked for prayers. You may ask for general prayers from the people participating, though, and thus include someone you know who's in need of help. I know my friend has cancer, but she hasn't asked us to pray for her, so I asked our sweat lodge group to remember all those in our prayers who are suffering from cancer. When the rocks were in, the door was once again closed, and four more songs were sung, while water was ladled onto the rocks. The dark and heat become easier to experience. A sort of routine has developed, and participants were much more relaxed. When the door opened again, we had more time to talk as more rocks were brought in. Others who hadn't spoken the first time had another opportunity to share.

The third round of the ceremony can be done in different ways. It can be thought of as the time when you focus on your community as an adult, and you can pray about strengthening that group. It is sometimes called "the women's round." Only women will sing the four songs. I sang my songs in this round, and we prayed for the women in our lives. The third round is also called "the healing round." A community member asked for help and was cared for by Robertjohn. He used mud collected from a spiritual place in the Owens Valley. The patients rubbed it on themselves like a liniment. Then Robertjohn ran eagle feather fans across their body to remove the disease and bad spirits. Finally, he used an eagle bone whistle to call in the spirit helpers to aid the sick person.

The lodge community sang as this ritual was performed. As one who has participated in this method of healing, I know the part of it that makes it work is that it's a powerful psychological tool to have the community focused on your needs, praying for your recovery, and sympathetic to your suffering. After the four songs were sung and the round was finished, the door was opened again. We cooled down and rested while the remaining rocks from the fire were brought in.

The fourth and last round of the sweat lodge ceremony is called "the old age round." This is a time to think about how you will do two things in old age: teach and give thanks for everything. Robertjohn called on four people to sing the songs of thanks. This round was pretty tough. All the rocks were in, and the heat was overwhelming. We struggled to stay focused. Robertjohn reminded us that there are only two roads in climbing the mountain of life, the easy one and the hard one. As you ascend the road, the easy way is to jump off the road. One feels free when they are falling off the cliff, but sooner or later, they will hit the bottom, hard. The hard road doesn't get easier; the mountain is always steep and difficult, but the one who walks it becomes stronger. "Stay awake," he says, "or go to sleep." "If you are awake, you cannot deny the truth." There is so much to think about after this long ceremony and so much to be grateful for. When the songs finished, we were told to bless ourselves again, and the door was opened one final time.

As we left lodge, we were once again told to give the fire outside an offering of tobacco. We quickly changed our clothes and went to the house for a shared feast, a pot-luck event, and everyone was eager to eat. The sweat ceremony lasted many hours, and everyone had worked up a great thirst and appetite. Before anyone ate, a "spirit plate" was prepared with a bit of all the foods to offer the spirits by burning it in the fire. We felt starved, and the lesson here was patience as we waited for all the participants to wander up to the house. The men came last since they needed to roll up the sides of the lodge, put away the tools, and put the fire out.

There are always some specific foods available after a ceremony. Robertjohn told us the spirits like meat, gravy, bread, berries, and coffee. Tonight, we stretched the interpretation by having a rich chicken pozole soup, in which the broth counted as the gravy. I had baked fresh homemade bread and made homemade blueberry pie. With freshly brewed coffee, the aroma was heavenly. We all assembled and said a prayer of thanks and dug in. It was a social time with plenty of laughter and fun.

Finally, full and exhausted, everyone pitched in to tidy up. We had put out the fire, folded up chairs, and cleaned the kitchen. The community gradually dispersed, and all was quiet on the ranch until the next ceremony. After the last person left, I thought about the ceremony as a professional anthropologist from my scientific perspective because I was intrigued by it. I saw how this ritual functions to create our cooperative, caring community. I also realized that the people who participate together are bound together by an intense physical trial. By sharing intimate stories and problems, we experienced psychological healing not unlike what occurs in counseling. Many people in our community also believe the physiological changes in the body are healthy due to heavy sweating, which rids the body of toxins as sauna advocates believe. Part of me knows through experience that much of what happens in the lodge can't be explained in rational terms. Everyone who participates gives it their own name, whether one calls it religious, supernatural, spiritual, or just plain magic. There's just something that happens to me after a sweat lodge ceremony experience that can't be understood as a scientist. There is some deep, ancestral part of me that craves community and ritual, and the sweat ceremony satisfies those needs in me. It just feels good, and I enjoy it, and so I will continue to be an avid participant. The first light of early dawn peeked through my window as I finally got to bed and drifted off into a peaceful sleep.

Sweat lodge at Black Widow Ranch

Building the sweat lodge

Ceremony day at the sweat lodge. Mario tending the fire

Robertjohn Knapp, ceremonial leader in a more recent photo.

Me and Robertjohn on a ceremony day

JUST KEEP GOING

CHAPTER 31

I had an epiphany in the sweat lodge one time. A word came to me, "tenacity." It's my survival word. It's now my favorite word. I remember the first time someone used that word. I sat in the office of my high-school counselor, Mrs. Rogers. She told me that I could do anything I wanted if I had "tenacity." I wasn't sure what that meant at the time, but I knew I was going to get tenacity because I had goals of being an actress and no one was going to stop me. The dictionary says, being tenacious is holding fast, being highly retentive, or being pertinacious, persistent, stubborn, or obstinate. If it was about sticking to it, and doing it, then I knew that was my destiny. I can credit my mother for that lesson.

In the lodge, I thought of a story about my mother when I was young. Although she had her faults, she had her qualities. One time, when I was a little girl, she took us to the beach to go grunion hunting. It was a magical experience. We headed out to the waves in the night with flashlights and buckets. The moon was high, and the foam on the crashing waves glowed with the moon's reflection in the blackness. There were other people on the beach, and everyone laughed all around us as we waited. A call up the beach told us that they were coming. Soon, fish were flopping everywhere in the receding tide. My mother yelled at us to grab them. We had to get them with our hands. I was scared and excited, rushing to the fish as fast as I could. The slippery silver bodies were small, just big enough for child-sized hands. We laughed and sang as we filled our buckets and then headed back home.

The next morning, we were shown how to clean the fish. We each only did two or three. We had to cut off the heads. There was gooey smelly stuff, and we didn't like how the fish felt slimy. The gutting was most disgusting to us. My mother did most of it. She then fried up the first batch, and we ate them. They were delicious. After eating our fill, we could see there were many left over that still needed to be cleaned. My mother went back to the duty of cleaning the remaining fish, so the uncooked leftover ones could be frozen for the future. There were so many in all those buckets of fish we had enthusiastically collected. I watched my mother work as I colored in my coloring book. I saw her continue on while I watched my favorite Saturday morning cartoon. She was still cleaning fish when I went outside to play. After a while in the yard, I returned to get a drink and saw my mother still cleaning those darn fish. I wished we had not collected so many. It seemed like she would be there all day.

After lunch, though, I noticed that the job was done. The fish had been wrapped in tin foil and placed in our big freezer in the garage. My mom never complained about the task, and I wondered how she could keep at that awful job for so long. We enjoyed the fish for some time, and I was grateful she had "tenacity."

Another thought came to me. It would dawn on me that tenacity was one of my defining characteristics. I am thoroughly convinced that the only reason I finished my graduate degrees was because I was determined to finish. I had stopped caring about the project and the research long before the task was done. I wasn't going to stop, though, until I was done, so I completed my work and earned my degrees.

I have been tenacious in continuing with life and grasping on to opportunities to thrive. I am convinced sometimes you just have to keep doing the regular things you do. There is therapy in routine. "Carry on," the saying goes. With this tenacious approach to life, I've been fortunate to meet the people I've met, like Geoff, my high-school crush. I have been to exotic places I never dreamed I would go because I believed I could, like Spain, Madagascar, and the Arctic. The experiences I've had were sometimes extraordinary, simply because I did not give up, like earning my Ph.D. and owning a ranch. I know I will be tenacious in all my pursuits until the end.

SUNSET

CHAPTER 32

John was out walking on the ranch after work. He sent me a text:

It's going to be a good sunset. I'll meet you out front.

We have a few lawn chairs in the front yard of the house, and over the last few years, we've regularly gone and sat together for these spectacular light shows. It's a bonding ritual, and it has helped heal our relationship.

"Ray will be graduating high school next month," John said.

"I just bought some nice slacks and a new shirt for him. At least we jumped through that hurdle," I said. I thought about how many times Ray had been suicidal, and all those appointments with psychiatrists, doctors, and school counselors. Ray's male identity was becoming normal for me.

I was also thinking about the future because Ray didn't have plans. He would either get a job or go to community college because doing nothing was not an option. Because of the psychological stress Ray had dealing with gender dysphoria, his grades suffered. He got D's and F's. Ray is happier and more motivated now, I thought. I was confident that everything would be okay in college.

It's only been a little over six months since Ray started using hormones, and he has already displayed a few physical changes. I noticed that he has new facial hair. Although it was at the peach-fuzz-looking stage, it made him very happy. His mastectomy was scheduled, and soon he would be able to legally change his name and gender on eighteenth birthday. His attitudes and manners are calmer and more mature. He has been attending a transgender counseling group meeting bi-monthly and making new friends. One of his friends comes to the house regularly and that has made the whole phenomenon of transgender more normal for me. I've changed too. I have gotten used to the idea that I didn't just lose a daughter, I gained a fine son. Ray is very generous to his friends. He never forgets birthdays or holiday gifts. He regularly chats with his friends who are in crises and loves animals with a passion equal to mine.

When you have a transgendered child, there are so many questions for the parents. Some things are out of your control and difficult to accept on many days. I often feel responsible, guilty, like I did something wrong. Maybe I could have eaten differently during my pregnancy? Maybe I wasn't a good role model for him growing up? I know it's useless to beat myself up, since only the present is my reality.

My training in anthropology taught me that in genetics, there is not just the simple XX and XY sex chromosome dichotomy that many assume. There is often aneuploidy, or having a different number of chromosomes, occurring at the sex chromosome position. Sometimes, there's XXY, XYY, XXX, or just one X, among other combinations. Sometimes, there are developmental mutations that can affect body and brain growth. I remember reading about the mutation of the Guevedoces in the Dominican Republic where boys do not develop into boys until puberty. Sometimes, there are environmental exposures that can affect growth and development. In fact, the physical differences between what we think of as male and female are not discrete ones, but continuous ones, with some people having physical traits that are ambiguous. Today, we call these individuals intersex people. Gender, or the way we think of ourselves, is a function of the brain, and it is also on a continuum. There are people today in our communities who see themselves even having fluid gender identity. Somedays they feel like a male, and somedays they feel like a female. It's not a fad, to think of oneself that way, but something that's been documented in the ethnographic records for over a hundred years.

Regardless of whether Ray's change was caused by genetics or environment, the situation is a natural one and isn't going away. I focus on the positive and the present. Even if Rebecca is gone, I have to remind myself that my son, Ray, is compassionate, strong-willed, and kind. We still have the same worries about our child's future that any parent would have, of course. Like everything I have lived through, somehow, I have adjusted to him though, and having Ray as a son is even starting to feel normal. I've evolved too, because I learned that this is a process for me as well and that it takes time for me to adjust.

"Look at those colors tonight!" John said.

I saw the pinks and oranges in the puffy clouds fade into reds and purples as the sky darkened.

John took my hand and smiled.

"Look!" I said, "There's a bat. I love how they dart around eating up those mosquitoes."

We watched the bat acrobat and saw others join it. I felt a pang of emotion. I realized it was peace and contentment, rare feelings for me. I could get used to that.

We watched as the sky blackened before we went inside.

Black Widow Ranch

John, Ray, and me on our 25th anniversary during COVID pandemic. We couldn't celebrate with a party, so we just went to the meadow in the mountains where we were married. So glad we made it this far and happily adjusted.

Me and my children

Me and John

Black Widow Ranch

EPILOGUE

I was born on an interesting day in history. The Dodgers and Yankees faced each other in the World Series. It was game five, and Don Larsen of the Yankees was pitching. He pitched a perfect game. That means no batter from the Dodgers ever got to first base in the nine innings. It is, to this day, the only time in baseball history to have occurred in a post-season game. It was an extraordinary feat.

As a baseball fan, I visited the Baseball Hall of Fame one year and looked for their exhibit about the event. When I found it, I was deeply impacted by the message the exhibit promotes. The museum placard notes that Don Larsen was not considered to be an extraordinary player. In fact, he never really did anything else important in his baseball career. Their message is this: Even ordinary people can do extraordinary things. I tell my students about it every semester. I want them to know that even if they don't have very high self-esteem or think they will never achieve star status in any career, they too can do something extraordinary.

As I hear more and more stories from students about their lives, it becomes clear to me that we all struggle and experience trials and difficulties throughout our lives. We are all normal, in the sense that this is what humans usually do. Maybe even now, the crazy experiences we all have is the zeitgeist of our times. Normal, or ordinary, doesn't mean we can't do extraordinary things.

Ray transferred to UC Riverside from community college and graduated after finishing his bachelor's education requirements.

He is working on his master's degree in library science. He will eventually move on with his life, and John and I will be living alone. We will adjust to the "empty nest" and return our focus to each other. I'm hopeful that we will continue to share our life together for some time. I don't know what the future holds, but I think since we both love to travel, there will be many new adventures for us. Our lives will always be full of complications and difficulties, which we will overcome if history is a good indicator. That's all okay with me.

I may not have had an easy life, and I may never have one in the future. I hear the words of Robertjohn in my head, "Pain is our teacher." To me, my whole life is a teacher, and so far with all these experiences I've had, it has shaped me. I feel compelled to teach what I have learned. That's what we humans do, share our knowledge, and expand on it. The most important lesson I have learned is that every human is unique, and because of that, we are all extraordinary. My childhood dream of being normal will always be a fantasy. There is no hope for normal, and not normal is what I will always be; maybe I will even be extraordinary.

Display at Baseball Hall of Fame for Don Larsen's perfect World Series game on day I was born.

ACKNOWLEDGMENTS

How do you thank all those who were part of the journey in creating this book? This was more than a decade long project, and there were plenty of steps and lessons along the way. Please forgive me if I fail to mention your name. There are so many more that often encouraged me or gave me advice than I've listed, but I appreciate you all.

I started to write my memoir because I had a creative writing student, Cliff Ashpaugh, taking my anthropology course. I regularly told my life stories in my class. He was enchanted by them and told me to write them down. Coming from a science background, and never having a creative writing course, I found the challenge daunting. He told me about a local writing group, the Coffee House Writing Group, I could attend. I felt out of my element when I got there. At the same time, I also felt inspired by the enthusiasm of the local writers. Cliff then encouraged me to attend the Writers Weekend, now called Culturama, at our college. The organizer Professor John Brantingham, and others, gave me some confidence to continue. I decided to enroll in a memoir writing workshop, hosted by Jo Scott-Coe, a creative writing professor and author in Riverside. I fell in love with the process and was determined to get my story down. Another source of endless encouragement was a colleague of mine in the biology department where I worked, Lynda Hoggan. She was writing her own memoir and soon we attempted to join other local writing groups looking for support and feedback on our efforts. Finally, finding Juanita Mantz in one of these groups we created our own group, the Tres Libras Writing Group, since we all have October birthdays. Together we met regularly for years over pizza, wine, laughter and tears and each created our books. I love these women like sisters and could not have created this work without them. I also often reached out to other successful local writers in the community for feedback. But a special thanks goes to my friend and part-time English professor, John Pinson. He assisted me, chapter by chapter, in fine tuning the ideas and organization.

Finally, with a draft in hand I reached out to Inlandia Institute in Riverside to look for a publisher. Cati Porter and Mark Givens were kind enough to invite me into their new 909 Books Collective to achieve this dream. I was excited to join the first cohort with participant Jacqueline Mantz to get this project finished. Jackie is the best; she is such a kind and hardworking human. Thank you for holding hands together to get our books done. Truly the world needs more people like these new 909 friends, who encourage, laugh, and devote untold hours of their lives to promoting our craft and helping the world hear valuable stories.

I want to thank others outside the writing community, as well. Of course, my family at first was tolerant of all my home meetings and efforts, and although they were hesitant in their support of me sharing our personal family stories, they came to understand the value in helping others feel that they are not alone. We are all just humans, just trying to figure out this journey called life, and no one has a road map or a game plan.

I want to thank some organizations that are important to me, as well. The Human Rights Campaign, Lambda Legal, and the American Civil Liberties Union are all outstanding groups where I regularly send my donations. They stand behind the LGBTQ+ community ensuring that all people are given the constitutional rights to which they are entitled. I find these groups inspiring and supportive of families like mine. Their support is essential in the different political climates that can be adversary that we must sometimes endure.

I would like to thank my family for their existence. I am eternally grateful to my husband John, and children, Rachael, James and Ray, for their encouragement, their patience in dealing with moody me and for always giving me unconditional love. I love you all.

Lastly, thank you to my mom and dad, long gone. I am grateful for the unique life you gave me.

ABOUT THE AUTHOR

Francesca Borella is a biological anthropologist who lives with her family at the Black Widow Ranch in Riverside, California. After years of teaching college students and telling stories from her life, and with the many requests from students and friends, Francesca turned to memoir and poetry. This is her debut.

THE 909 BOOKS COLLECTIVE

909 Books is an independent publisher with the experience of two leading regionally-based publishers behind it. **The 909 Books Collective** is a unique mentorship model that relies on its members to ensure mutual success. The exclusivity and vetting of authors/members ensures that all 909 Books publications meet the highest standards of book publishing.

WWW.909BOOKS.COM

www.ingramcontent.com/pod-product-compliance
Lightning Source LLC
LaVergne TN
LVHW010649110826
845149LV00014B/3009

* 9 7 8 1 9 6 2 7 0 2 0 0 3 *